HOW
LEADERS
SPEAK

HOW LEADERS SPEAK

Essential Rules for Engaging and Inspiring Others

JIM GRAY

DUNDURN PRESS
TORONTO

Project Editor: Michael Carroll
Editor: Nicole Chaplin
Designer: Jennifer Scott
Printer: Webcom

Library and Archives Canada Cataloguing in Publication

Gray, Jim, 1950-
    How leaders speak : essential rules for engaging and inspiring
others / by Jim Gray.

ISBN 978-1-55488-701-9

1. Business communication. 2. Communication in management. 3. Oral communication.
I. Title.

HF5718.G739 2010   658.4'52   C2009-907458-3

    2   3   4   5   14   13   12   11

We acknowledge the support of the Canada Council for the Arts and the Ontario Arts Council for our publishing program. We also acknowledge the financial support of the Government of Canada through the Book Publishing Industry Development Program and The Association for the Export of Canadian Books, and the Government of Ontario through the Ontario Book Publishers Tax Credit program, and the Ontario Media Development Corporation.

Care has been taken to trace the ownership of copyright material used in this book. The author and the publisher welcome any information enabling them to rectify any references or credits in subsequent editions.

J. Kirk Howard, President

Printed and bound in Canada.
www.dundurn.com

Dundurn Press	Gazelle Book Services Limited	Dundurn Press
3 Church Street, Suite 500	White Cross Mills	2250 Military Road
Toronto, Ontario, Canada	High Town, Lancaster, England	Tonawanda, NY
M5E 1M2	LA1 4XS	U.S.A. 14150

How Leaders Speak is dedicated
to the memory of my parents,
Bertie and Jimmy Gray,
inspiring communicators both.

Contents

Author's Note

The ability to speak convincingly to others — to compel them — has to rank as one of the most important skills in business and in life.

It's the mark of a true leader.

For many who aspire to leadership, it's the one proficiency they lack. For many who occupy positions of leadership, it's the one missing element that prevents them from fully realizing all that they can be.

Audiences in today's communication-saturated age — consumers, voters, employees, shareholders, and the media — are more demanding and critical than ever. They want leaders who can address them with clarity and authenticity.

You are being judged

You don't have to be running a Fortune 500 company to be scrutinized on your presentation skills. Whoever you are and whatever you do, you're continually being evaluated by how well you speak — how credibly, how naturally, and how enthusiastically.

In fact, listeners will come to all sorts of conclusions about the type of person you are based on how effectively you address them. Sounds unfair, doesn't it?

What if you suffer from overwhelming nervousness, or speak English as a second language, or simply happen to be having one of those off days when your delivery isn't as sharp as you'd like it to be?

It doesn't matter. You're going to be judged all the same.

Now, here's the great news. You can learn how to speak in a way that engages and inspires your audience.

You can learn how to speak like a leader.

Whatever your background or vocation — whether you're an executive, homemaker, or student — if you're committed to becoming an accomplished presenter and you're willing to do the work, you can achieve the goal of consistently speaking with excellence.

And it won't matter if you're addressing hundreds of delegates at a conference, a few dozen attendees at a PTA meeting, or a pair of classmates at school. You'll be forging a powerful connection with your listeners.

About this book

How Leaders Speak covers the five keys to speaking like a leader: preparation, certainty, passion, engagement, and commitment. It includes advice and insider tips on everything from organizing speeches and presentations quickly and efficiently, to overcoming nervousness and issuing a strong call to action.

Consider this book your comprehensive guide on how to shine whatever the presentation opportunity — whether it's an important address, a crucial new business pitch, or a big media interview.

Throughout it all, consider me your personal communication skills coach.

What qualifies me to write a book on speaking like a leader?

First, communication is my passion. For more than twenty years, I've been privileged to help hundreds of people, from CEOs and senior politicians to unemployed youth, in their pursuit of the better presentation, the deeper audience connection, the memorable quote.

From my coaching experience I can tell you this: great speakers are made, not born. It's simply a matter of finding the leader within.

The mistakes I have made

The second reason that qualifies me to write this book is that I've learned from hard personal experience, having made every conceivable error in the presentation skills universe, and then some.

I've shared your pain.

We all make mistakes. We can all fall short, in every endeavour in life.

There's something particularly humiliating, though, about failing in a presentation, whether it's in front of two people or two thousand. It's as if the whole world has stopped to watch and say, "What a loser."

The derision invariably comes from inside our own heads.

After a bad speech, or even an embarrassing moment in a speech, you may feel like you never want to interact with another human being again. Go ahead and feel that way, for a little while.

Then you need to get productive — analyze the reasons for the slip-up, ascertain how you can avoid repeating it, and get right back on that communication horse.

That's how you get better.

That's how you learn to speak like a leader.

The right to express ourselves publicly in a democratic society, to freely convey our ideas and opinions, is a gift, among the finest bestowed upon the human race.

A lot of people fought to give us this gift. We owe them our best.

So let's get started by examining the five keys to speaking like a leader.

The five keys. They'll equip you to excel as a presenter, even when the odds appear to be stacked heavily against you.

The five keys. They'll help you open career doors that seemed forever closed, and facilitate your ascension to the next level.

The five keys. They're how leaders speak.

Jim Gray
Toronto, Ontario
January 2010

The First Key — Preparation

How's this for a high-pressure scenario?

Your CEO steps into your office and gives you some big news. She's chosen you to deliver a keynote presentation at a major conference, "Industry 2020," in two months in Las Vegas. Basically, the deal is this: she wants you to share the company's vision with more than five hundred senior and mid-level executives from throughout North America, with the goal of generating excitement about your organization's planned initiatives and, ideally, renewed respect for your solid but staid outfit.

YOUR BIG SPEAKING OPPORTUNITY

Congratulations. You've just been given an opportunity to speak like a leader to leaders.

You're pleased and excited, right?

Perhaps your overriding emotion is fear. You know for a fact that the CEO, let's call her Peggy, should be the natural choice to give this presentation.

But Peggy has made the decision to sit this one out. She's received extensive media coverage recently, and feels that a cult of personality has been starting to develop around her.

To her credit, she wants to put more of the focus back on the company and its strong senior management team. And you, my friend, are a member in good standing of that team.

You suspect, though, that one of your colleagues, your chief rival and longtime nemesis, the widely reviled Tim, would be a better choice to deliver the presentation. He knows a lot more about the company vision. The sycophantic Tim is also tighter with the CEO, but Tim will be in Europe for some strategic planning meetings during "Industry 2020" and those meetings can't be rescheduled.

So while Tim is slogging away in overcast Berlin, you'll be basking in the spotlight in sunny Vegas.

Who says good things don't happen to good people?

It is what it is

Now, a cynic might say that you're the third choice to give the big presentation at "Industry 2020," and the cynic might be right.

But it should make absolutely no difference.

Whether you were choice number one or twenty-one, you've been handed the ball. Now you have to run with it.

Put any negative self-talk out of your head and tell yourself here and now that you're going to take this project on, and complete it superbly.

Not to overwhelm you, but following your thirty-minute presentation you'll be asked to take questions from the audience. Relax — it's all good.

If you're not pleased and excited, you should be. You get to serve the informational needs of a prestigious audience, while enhancing your company and personal profile. It doesn't get much better than that.

Few learned skills carry with them the potential to speed you up the corporate, educational, and political food chains faster than the ability to speak effectively to others.

Barack Obama, the forty-fourth president of the United States, is the most dramatic modern example of the career-building power of speech. Just think about it: Obama was an Illinois State senator, little known nation-ally, when he rocked the 2004 Democratic National Convention with his passionate keynote. Four years and four months later, he was elected president.

Chances are you aren't planning on running for the leadership of the Free World, but you can employ the simple but powerful speaking techniques that Mr. Obama uses to compel his audiences.

We're going to assume that you've enthusiastically accepted the invitation from your CEO to present at "Industry 2020," and thanked her for the opportunity.

Good move. Now, let's get to work.

Thinking about the challenge

How do you even begin to get your head around such an assignment? By embracing the first and most important key to speaking like a leader: preparation.

I've been a presentation skills coach for a long time, and it became apparent to me early on that accomplished communicators have three qualities in common.

First, they consider the chance to address others freely in a public forum to be an occasion to be respected, and never taken lightly.

Second, they understand that a presentation needs to be more than a compilation of facts, figures, and opinion but rather a story, the most powerful and sublime form of communication.

Finally, they're rigorous and disciplined in their preparation.

Skilled presenters spend a great deal of time thinking about who their listeners are, what those listeners know, and what they need to know in order to respond positively to the message being delivered.

They know a presentation shouldn't be about them. It should be about the people who show up to hear them.

Traumatic listener experiences

The need to consider the audience would undoubtedly come as a surprise to many of the speakers I covered as a young business reporter, back in the day. I heard a lot of bad speeches — mumbled, disorganized, meandering, interminable, and ultimately incomprehensible discourses that sorely tested the patience of the inconceivably polite people in attendance.

More often than not, the speakers knew little or nothing about the background or mindset of those in their audiences, and didn't really seem to care. They'd mispronounce the names of the executives hosting the event at which they were appearing, propagate a dated or ignorant view of the issues affecting the sponsoring organization, and talk incessantly and reverentially about themselves.

It wasn't pretty.

These speakers weren't just rude, they were confusing. As a journalist, it was my responsibility to make sense of the just-completed assault on rationality. Because the presenters weren't always available for interviews following their remarks and because I had to produce a story, regardless of whether a speech warranted coverage or not (it often didn't), I was left to grapple with a perplexing question: what was their point?

Out of this early career tribulation came the determination to devote my professional existence to coaching good-hearted men and women in the preparation and delivery of presentations with clarity.

Clarity comes about only as a result of understanding — understanding your audience, its issues, its attitudes, and its motivations. Without knowing all of this, you simply won't be successful. You can't be successful.

Audiences can tell, astonishingly quickly, whether speakers have taken the time to learn anything about them or not.

When speakers have done their due diligence, listeners can be remarkably supportive and forgiving. When they haven't, well, onlookers can become downright hostile, in a silent, seething way that can take on a near-malevolent force of its own.

But you'll never experience such antipathy, because you're all about the preparation.

Or soon will be.

GETTING STARTED

You can begin preparing for your big presentation by thinking about others. How can your remarks at "Industry 2020" best serve the informational needs of your listeners, while achieving the goal set down by your CEO?

Schedule an in-depth meeting with your boss and ensure that you share absolute agreement about the objective of the speech, an understanding of what success looks like, and her buy-in on the investment of time and resources it will take for you to adequately research, write, and rehearse the presentation.

You can't slack off on any of this stuff. Do that, and you're guaranteed to come up short in Las Vegas.

Schedule weekly meetings with your CEO to review your progress and to solicit her input. For this project, your personal motto should become, "There's no *I* in team."

Regular consultation will eliminate (or at least dramatically reduce) the chances of any frantic, late changes resulting from your boss not having seen the content, while providing you with the ongoing benefit of her insights and advice.

Comprehensive preparation includes several essential components, including learning as much as possible about those to whom you'll be speaking.

You need to know about your audience

For whatever reason, presenters at every level often fail to embrace this responsibility with the diligence and care it so obviously requires. It's as if they believe they'll somehow learn too much about their listeners, and the knowledge will serve to spoil the spontaneity of their presentation.

But that's just crazy. You simply can't know too much about your audience.

Put in a call to the conference organizers and learn about the delegates who'll be attending "Industry 2020." What organizations do they represent? What are their expectations of the conference, and from your presentation?

Ask for a delegate list, and for permission to contact a handful of respected attendees. You'll want them to answer your questions candidly.

Ask:

"What are the biggest challenges facing our sector?"

"What keeps you up at night?"

Don't be reluctant to go deeper when you sense there's more to learn. You can always ask, "Can you tell me more?"

Your aim should be to acquire enough quality information to understand the attitude of your audience at "Industry 2020." It's invaluable intelligence to keep in mind as you build a presentation that tells your story while exceeding the expectations of your listeners.

Think about life from their perspective. These days, the people who run businesses are quicker than ever to dismiss or ignore information that doesn't relate to their organization's most pressing needs, whether short or long-term.

Business leaders are more focused than ever. They have to be. They want insights and ideally some answers,

yet very few speakers provide them. So be a speaker
with the insights.

Be a speaker with the answers.

Find — or create — the "nugget"

Resolve to discover and present at least one "nugget"
of information that your listeners don't know, or may
have overlooked. It will get their attention — and boost
your credibility.

Can't find the nugget? Then create it.

Take the initiative. You'll want to get permission
from your CEO and the conference organizers first, but
once they're onside, survey the attendees about an issue
that will be central to your speech. Then present the
results, with appropriate theatrics, at "Industry 2020."

The nugget concept also works effectively for internal presentations.

Say you're given the assignment of presenting to
your senior management team. Again, assuming the
approval of your CEO, you could poll a select number
of customers about the company's new national advertising campaign, or your co-workers about an internal
productivity program, for example.

In fact, when preparing new business pitches,
well-run public relations and advertising agencies will
frequently survey captive respondents — their own
employees — to collect research on a prospective client's

products or service, and then present the findings at their pitch. It's an inexpensive but effective way of proving to the prospect that the agency is willing to go the extra mile to learn about its business and contribute to its success. Prospects love it. They're flattered by the attention, and often learn something of solid value about their business.

Will the results of your informal survey be scientific or statistically relevant? Absolutely not.

Will the members of your audience be interested in them? Absolutely.

Why? Because the findings will be all about them.

The right nugget can help you shoot the lights out at "Industry 2020."

Are you getting a little more excited about your big presentation now?

Is Vegas a party town?

UTILIZING THE POWER OF THREE

You've learned about your audience, which will prove invaluable in your speech, the telling of your story.

But just what will that story be?

In these early days, you need to establish a theme for your talk, one that your boss endorses (the more enthusiastically, the better), the organizers approve, and you love.

You're going to be spending a lot of time with your theme. It's the core of your presentation and you should be able to express it in a single, concise statement that anyone can understand. If you don't have a theme, you won't have a speech. All you'll have is verbiage, disconnected and ineffectual.

Once you've established your approved theme, it's time to start creating your presentation, your story.

Most speakers make this process far too complicated, when all they really need to do is employ a simple but unerringly effective template known as the Power of Three.

A remarkable number

There's something quite special about the number three. From an early age, we organize, explain, and retain information best when it's arranged in threes.

Children instinctively "get" the number three. Indeed, kids are often better communicators than adults because they're invariably sure about what they want, and they think and speak in threes. Free of all the complexities that mark adult lives, they haven't matured to the point where they fear simplicity. They embrace it.

Great speakers of the adult variety welcome simplicity as well.

It can set you apart.

It's been said that never have we known more and understood less. We live in a world flooded with information, yet executives generally speak less effectively than ever. Swimming in data, they try to cut through the dross to deliver relevant content that hits the mark.

Much of the time they fail. Why?

They're insecure about their content.

The reason so many presentations and pitches go over their allotted time these days — an appalling breach of professional etiquette called "overspeaking" — is that speakers are often uncertain about what should comprise a story, so they pile in every piece of even tenuously related information in order to support it.

It's little wonder they go long.

Great communication starts with making the right decisions about what material needs to go into your presentation and what needs to stay out, given the time available.

The Power of Three helps you make the right decisions. It's an elementary formula that facilitates the organization of material, however complex, within three main categories: Introduction, Body, and Conclusion.

Let's examine each category and determine how to best employ it.

The Introduction

The introduction easily qualifies as the most critical part of your presentation. It's here where you either hook your listeners, or let them know they're going to be in for a banal or disagreeable experience.

Or both.

Presentations often go off the rails right out of the gate because the speaker never lets the audience members know what's in it for them. At the outset, a presenter needs to state, "This is why what I'm about to tell you is important to you."

I often ask clients, "What's everyone's favourite radio station?"

Why, it's WIIFM, of course: What's in It for Me?

It's how every audience member thinks. It's the way we all think, for the most part, just about all of the time.

Hit your listeners right off the top with how they'll benefit from your talk, how it will help their careers, their organizations, or both. Be as specific as possible.

Audiences, for the most part, are remarkably keen on having you succeed, if only for self-interest. They know that if the talk tanks, it's bound to be an unsettling occasion for all concerned.

If you don't engage your listeners early — within the first ninety seconds — you won't get them at all. Some will continue to try to make a connection between your topic and their lives, but most will tune out, their heads bowed before their PDAs.

Make sure you hook them right out of the gate.

Context is key

The introduction is where you state your theme, and do what so few speakers do (at least well): provide context.

Context is the most valuable and under-utilized ingredient of modern day communication. Just as a building needs a solid foundation to remain upright, so presentations require the underpinning of context or background to stand firm and soar.

With context, you can speak like a leader by setting the groundwork for the information to come, while supplying listeners with an account that reflects your perspective.

Often, speakers wrongly assume that listeners have the most current information on the issue at hand (or already share the speakers' views on it). As a result, presenters will begin their story at, say, point D, when the audience doesn't know, understand, or fully appreciate the consequences of A, B, or C. If you don't lay down the back story, your listeners will be struggling to catch up with you for the duration of your presentation.

When you fail to supply adequate background you shortchange your listeners, since it's unlikely everyone will have updated, comprehensive knowledge of a subject or issue.

Ensuring everyone is up to speed

Unless you know for certain that the audience already shares your level of knowledge or experience, you have to lay down context. If some listeners are fully up to speed on a subject and others aren't, you need to serve the ones who aren't by reviewing the issue (quickly and efficiently) from the beginning. Otherwise, you run the risk of losing them.

As for those who already know the latest score, well, they'll just have to sit through your review. It's no big deal. Usually, no one minds hearing the same information more than once; it can actually be reassuring in this manic world.

There are other important reasons for providing clarifying context in the introduction. If done well, with at least a modicum of objectivity, you can start influencing an audience's perception of an issue. Listeners will begin to see the matter from your standpoint because, through your discourse, they've shared your experience.

Finally, laying down lean, well-structured context makes you look smart and self-assured. It means that you care enough about your listeners to ensure they have all the information they require to fully understand your story. It means you've taken the time to bring about understanding. It means you're speaking like a leader.

The Body

At the heart of the Power of Three, the body is where you expand on your theme, and make your major points. But if it becomes overloaded, the body is also where presentations can fall apart.

Your listeners always need to know where you are — and where you're going — in the telling of your story. An efficient way to keep them on track is, again, through the magic number three.

Too often the body becomes a repository for a laundry list of observations and initiatives. As a longtime media trainer I can tell you that journalists' attention drops way off after three points; it's the same with every audience.

For example, here's a statement you could make in a media interview that would get a reporter's attention: "Our programs are valuable to the community for three reasons: one, they create employment; two, they save taxpayers money; and three, they benefit the environment."

Employ that tight, bright media technique to arrange the body of your presentation in threes. If it's essential that you cover off eight or ten points, organize them in categories or silos of three.

Of course, you can always choose to have only one or two points. Those options work as well.

But there's nothing like three. It's the power number.

The Conclusion

As a reporter, I covered a host of speeches that were quite successful up until the last few minutes, but then ended up as if they'd been accidentally dropped off a cliff.

A typical speaker would have concluded something like this, "Er, thank you for your attention. Ah, any questions?"

However you end, you need to do it with impact.

The conclusion is where you sum up, provide a resolution to the story you've just shared with the audience, and issue a specific call to action. What do you want your listeners to do after hearing your presentation? Buy your product? Sign up for your service? Invest in your company? Work together to make Canada a better place?

Unless you tell them, they won't know.

The conclusion presents you with a final opportunity to speak like a leader.

Everyone wants to know what's going to happen in the days, months, and years ahead. If you have an opinion about the future, a reasoned, thoughtful outlook, you can differentiate yourself from the many timid souls who disclose only what the audience already knows.

Write long, cut short

However you decide to tell your story at "Industry 2020," use the versatile Power of Three as your template.

For your first draft, write as long as you can, working in every conceivable fact, observation, and anecdote about your subject matter. It's a healthy, productive process that will get you thinking about the telling of your story in new ways, from different angles.

Now, edit ruthlessly. For every sentence, ask: "Do my listeners really need to know this? Will it be essential to their understanding of my story? Am I providing new, valuable, or insightful information?"

Those questions will help you quickly separate the narrative wheat from the chaff. After that, it's just a matter of placing the grain in the appropriate silo under the Power of Three template.

Life is complicated. Communication need not be.

Organizing Your Presentation According to the Power of Three

Introduction

- Hook your listeners early; why is what you're about to say important to them?
- State your theme.
- What context or background does the audience need to fully understand the information to come?

Body

- Arrange the core of your presentation here, in three or fewer points.
- Make it clear what point you're on, where you've been, and where you're going.
- Support each point (with one or more of the following: an anecdote, fact, example, quote, or insight).

Conclusion

- Provide resolution to your story.
- Issue a definitive call to action.
- End with impact — in content and delivery. Leave plenty of time between the conclusion of your formal remarks and your invitation for questions. Don't rush your listeners; give them an opportunity to express their appreciation of your presentation.

The "list" option

I'm an enthusiastic fan of the Power of Three for several reasons — among them is that it provides new, inexperienced speakers with a simple, easy-to-deploy template for organizing their narratives. Indeed, it serves presenters of all levels of know-how and ability exceptionally well.

Given their acumen, though, accomplished speakers certainly have license to deviate from the Power of Three to organize and deliver presentations in lists of up to ten elements.

Comedian David Letterman has popularized the "Top Ten" list, which can work superbly if the points are clearly themed (for example, Letterman's "Top Ten Text Messages Sent by Tiger Woods") and delivered with substantial flair.

If you believe you have the wherewithal to manage a list successfully, don't feel locked into the number ten. Lists from four to nine elements can work efficiently, too. But don't go over ten; at eleven, your presentation will start to feel and sound like the recital of a catalogue.

I conduct several workshops that are organized according to lists, among them "The Seven Most Powerful Ways to Influence Up," "The Seven Steps to An Effective Meeting," and "The Ten Biggest Communication Mistakes Financial Advisors Make."

If I were to speak on "The Communication Mistakes I've Made," I'd organize the talk according to the Power of Three.

Why? Some lists are just too distressing, for listeners and presenters alike.

"OVERSPEAK" AT YOUR OWN RISK

As you begin creating your presentation, you have to promise me that under no circumstances will you include so much content that you'll speak too long on your big day at "Industry 2020."

Those who talk over their limit are guilty of one of the most serious offences in communication: over-speaking.

It's abominable.

I once attended a conference where a succession of presenters crossed the line from mere self-absorption to lunacy.

Indifferent to the obvious distress of the audience, they each rambled interminably past their twenty-minute speaking times. One bore went on for forty-five minutes (yes, my friend, more than double the period apportioned) and asked for questions from the audience afterward. None were forthcoming.

By this time it was well past noon. The conference luncheon was delayed and served cold. The afternoon's speakers didn't get to eat much at all, because they were so busy hacking away at their presentations to comply with the edict of the now-desperate conference organizers to reduce the length of the talks to come. The proceedings ran late anyway. Flights were missed and delegates were apoplectic.

What overspeaking says

Here's the bottom line: When you overspeak, you're basically saying to your listeners, "Look, I know I'm over my time, and I know you're aggravated, and I know that the speakers to follow will have to cut their remarks short. But frankly, I'm more important than any of them, or any of you for that matter, so just sit back and listen to the genius that is me."

One might assume that less effective presenters would be more conscientious about delivering a presentation within the time assigned. In fact, the opposite is often true. Poor speakers, psychologically disconnected from their audience, can just plow on, struggling to get through a story that was absurdly long to begin with.

Whatever the reason — insensitivity or cluelessness — those who overspeak are paying a heavy price. Potential supporters and customers among an audience might reasonably wonder, "If this person can't fulfill a simple obligation, such as speaking for twenty minutes, why should I trust him to honour any other undertaking, like delivering a product on time, or completing a project within budget?"

Overspeaking drains time, reputations, and an audience's patience. So what can you do to avoid it? Plenty.

Make a commitment to speak *under* your time

Blaise Pascal, the seventeenth-century French math-
ematician, physicist, and philosopher, knew the potency
of brevity. "I have made this letter longer than usual," he
wrote, "because I lack the time to make it short."

Hundreds of years ago, Pascal nailed it.

Less is invariably more in communication. You've
been asked to speak for thirty minutes at "Industry
2020"; you should prepare your remarks for twenty-five.
Why? Presentations have a way of expanding in delivery,
what with introductions, technical glitches, and extem-
poraneous remarks.

By finishing slightly under time, you'll look — and
sound — like a leader. Go over by even a minute and
your credibility begins to suffer.

I love a presenter who, shortly after being introduced, will say, "I'm going to speak for twenty minutes, and then I'll be happy to take any questions. I
can guarantee you that we'll be done by 11:45 so we'll
have plenty of time to head out of here and get down
the hall to enjoy the delicious lunch that's being prepared for us."

With that, the speaker tells the audience members
that they're in good hands, so everyone tends to relax,
free of concerns about time, and listens.

Rehearse, and be ready to chop — or fill

How long you end up speaking at "Industry 2020" shouldn't come as a surprise, to you or your audience. You need to rehearse often, for a number of reasons.

First, the better you know your story, the freer you'll be to be yourself. Second, you'll come to know how long the different sections of your narrative run, which will be essential if you have to add or jettison material.

Why would you possibly have to add material? After all, isn't overspeaking a crime right up there with bad grammar and pastel leisure suits?

Yes, indeed.

However, you have to be prepared for anything in the presentation business, including the possibility that another speaker eats some bad salmon, takes ill, and bows out. Meanwhile, you're feeling fine; you had the chicken. But the conference organizers want you to lengthen your remarks.

Think about what information you can add, while maintaining the structural integrity of your talk and, more importantly, keeping the audience interested.

Say the previous speaker goes over his time, and in order for the proceedings to stay on track you have to chop eight minutes out of your presentation?

What would you take out? You need to know, ahead of time.

Almost always, the material that can be excised takes the form of supporting information in the body. You'd be hard-pressed to remove stuff from any other location.

Think about it. You'll need your entire introduction to compel your listeners, introduce your theme, and let them know what's in your remarks for them.

The conclusion is where you provide resolution and issue your call to action. You'll need all of that.

The content to go would have to come from the body. In rehearsal, shorten and lengthen the midsection to deliver different length versions of your presentation; try a version at twenty minutes, even forty-five. Have some fun with it.

It's far better to anticipate time-related challenges and prepare for them now, than half an hour before you take the lectern at "Industry 2020."

Join in the fight

It's straightforward. Your obligation as a speaker is to relate an absorbing story that serves the informational needs of your listeners within the time prescribed, and then sit down.

But you have another duty as well, and that's to help eliminate the scourge of overspeaking. To be eradicated for all time, it's got to be rendered socially unacceptable, like smoking in public buildings or watching reality TV.

I have a friend who, when taking the lectern to follow a speaker who's gone over his time, will say, "I was going to speak for twenty minutes, but unfortunately

Ed went on too long so I have only fifteen minutes to address you."

My friend doesn't smile when he says this. Neither does Ed.

For people like Ed, a presentation means never having to say you're finished. However, the days of those who partake in the self-indulgent practice of overspeaking are numbered.

The revolution has begun.

THE PERILS OF POWERPOINT

Will you use PowerPoint at "Industry 2020"?

Think carefully about your decision. There's a lot on the line.

I once described PowerPoint as the most misused technological innovation since the handgun. Why? It kills a lot of presentations.

In "PowerPoint Is Evil," a now-famous article in the September 2003 issue of *Wired* magazine, Edward Tufte compared slideware (computer programs like Power-Point) to an "expensive prescription drug that promised to make us beautiful but didn't. Instead the drug had frequent, serious side effects: It induced stupidity, turned everyone into bores, wasted time, and degraded the quality and credibility of communication."

With those words, Edward Tufte became my personal hero.

When used responsibly, PowerPoint can be a useful tool, bringing clarity and organization to the parts of speeches, presentations, and briefings that need it. Far more often than not, though, it's atrociously deployed.

Great speeches help build great careers, so I find it incomprehensible that so many presenters undercut the incredible personal power that comes from connecting deeply with an audience to throw up a collection of pedestrian slides and read aloud desultory, static information that listeners can whip through much faster.

Your PowerPoint slides should serve as a guide, not a script.

Hiding behind slides

I suspect the penchant for poorly delivered PowerPoint has to do with the fact that great numbers of presenters, even among the executive and professional sets, are unnerved by the preparation and discipline it takes to speak well in public.

When PowerPoint came along many of them figured, "This is terrific. Now I don't have to go through the hassle of writing and editing a script, which takes forever. After all, I've got a life going on here. I'll just organize a deck of slides covering the main points and address them one by one. It's all good!"

The advent of the now-ubiquitous technology served a deeper psychological need as well, seemingly protecting the fearful from the perceived oppressive scrutiny of audiences by diverting at least some attention away from a jittery speaker to visual aids.

But just as you can feel lonelier at a crowded party than in the solitude of your own bedroom, PowerPoint, badly utilized, can isolate and diminish you.

The purpose of PowerPoint

Folks, slideware was meant to support your presentations, not *become* them. The best speakers in the world rarely use it. They don't have to. They tell their stories the old-fashioned way, with an uplifting combination of words and passion.

It's no surprise that the higher you go up the corporate food chain, the less often tools like PowerPoint are used. There's a reason for that. The language of leaders typically doesn't translate to an inanimate screen.

As a presentation skills coach, I spend a good deal of time working with clients and their PowerPoint decks. I emphasize a simple ideology, and it's this: We humans get to run the technology. It doesn't get to run us.

That belief underpins my ten rules for using Power-Point.

Determine if you really need it

If some of your content — such as complex technical or financial data — requires slideware, so be it. But keep in mind that effective speakers give as much of themselves to their listeners as possible.

Perhaps your thirty-minute presentation can feature just fifteen minutes worth of slides, or even ten. Keep thinking of ways to reduce the number of slides, to give the audience more of you and fewer words, numbers, and graphs on a screen.

Make sure your use of PowerPoint is appropriate. For example, it has no place within communication that evokes strong emotion, such as the announcement of layoffs or expressions of sympathy. Here, listeners require the full human connection.

Make sure your story comes first

The best presentations result from the careful preparation of a written draft, from which your main points are extracted. You can then display and speak to those points.

The script comes first and the points second, not the other way around.

If you simply produce points and attempt to link them, your narrative will never be as smooth or as cohesive as it would be if you'd created your script first.

Presenters sometimes borrow, inherit, or are saddled with PowerPoint decks created by others. It's always difficult to tell someone else's story, even if it's one you're familiar with.

My advice here is to build a new introduction, before rolling into the slides, linking your experience and responsibilities with the material to come.

Try and make at least some of the story your own.

Don't overload your deck

Everyone has, at one time or another, been subject to an assault by a speaker displaying slides so laden with information as to be indecipherable. What does that say about the presentation and, more importantly, the presenter?

Not much.

It's simple: the more material you jam onto a deck, the harder it is for members of the audience to read (especially those at the back of the room) and the more challenging it becomes for you to present.

If you have detailed information you believe listeners require, include it in a handout.

This will make you look quite smart. You'll have, in fact, two versions of your slides: the comprehensive handout and the cleaner, eminently simpler presentation version, from which you'll speak.

Display three points per slide (remember our Power

of Three template), four maximum. The fewer words per point, the better.

For years, the generally accepted rule of thumb was to deliver one PowerPoint slide for every minute of delivery time. Skilled presenters can certainly cover off a slide in less than sixty seconds, especially if it doesn't require a ton of explanation, but the "one for one" rule still isn't a bad one to keep in mind.

For a thirty-minute presentation, thirty slides are plenty, unless you're a consummate raconteur with a tight, superbly well-choreographed show that moves the story along seamlessly. Most people don't operate at that level. And I always advise erring on the side of caution.

Go light on the slides, and heavy on your relationship with the audience.

Think symmetry

Speaking effectively is all about taking the pressure off yourself so you can be yourself.

Forget about any slide transitions for at least the first ninety seconds of your presentation. Instead, use that time to establish a bond with your listeners against the background of a slide featuring your organization's brand or logo.

Conclude your remarks with your brand or logo coming up again. It will communicate to your listeners that you're coming to your close, without you having to say "in conclusion" (please don't say "in conclusion," it's cliché) or "as I wrap up."

Presentation symmetry is a good thing.

It will make you look organized and, just as importantly, eliminate the need to ever create concluding slides that read, "Thank you" or "Questions?'

We're not in elementary school here. Let's have some dignity.

Maintain the connection

All over the world, presenters have fallen in love with PowerPoint and left their audiences behind in order to consummate the affair.

You've seen them, their backs to their stricken listeners, reading aloud some arcane reference from a slide groaning with data, the proceedings entirely comatose.

As a responsible speaker, it's essential that you begin and end each slide transition with eye contact to maintain your critical relationship with the audience. Once you've confirmed that the appropriate slide is in place (and you can do that by glancing down at your laptop, not turning around to gape at the screen behind you), "square up" to the crowd and begin speaking.

You can, of course, turn and refer to a slide, but not every slide. If there's something important on the screen you choose to emphasize, walk to it (backwards if you can; you want to minimize the time you have your back or even your side to an audience), and point to it, facing your listeners.

"Look at this," you might say. "Our sales were up 20 percent this quarter — let me tell you why."

See if you can do all this without a laser pointer, which can vibrate and shake in the hands of even slightly nervous presenters, and can distract listeners. There's an old saying in presentation skills: anything that distracts, detracts.

If you must hold a laser pointer, grasp it in your right hand and support it on your left forearm, or vice versa.

All slides aren't created equal; some will be more important than others. Nor will every point on a slide carry the same significance as others. Perhaps, on certain slides, you'll want to speak to only one point. That's cool. You're the one telling the story.

Be creative

Want to make an impact?

Embed a digital clip or two in your PowerPoint presentation. They can generate a great deal of impact when utilized well, but many speakers don't use them well.

They'll play a somnolent, self-serving twenty-minute feature on their organization's environmental initiatives and wonder why listeners are tromping off to the bar.

Solicit the opinions of respected peers on the suitability of your clips before playing them on presentation day. Will they enhance audience understanding in a captivating way, and in a reasonable amount of time? If so, in they go. If not, save them for the company retreat.

Use restraint

Just because we possess the technology to feature assorted elements of our every experience doesn't mean we should.

I once watched a speaker at a major conference, a widely respected professional, embarrass himself and his audience by including family photographs and cartoons in his PowerPoint presentation.

Someone should have reminded him that the speaking venue was a business function, and that his photos and caricatures were, well, unfortunate.

Clearly, he wasn't communicating like a leader.

Ten Rules for PowerPoint

1. Determine if you really need it.
2. Make sure your story comes first.
3. Keep thinking of ways to reduce the number of slides.
4. Aim for three points per slide — the fewer words per point the better.
5. Consider a presentation and handout version of your deck.

6. Think symmetry — with a title slide to open and close.

7. Utilize eye contact to introduce and conclude each slide.

8. Be creative — consider embedding digital clips.

9. Keep it professional.

10. Do not include "Thank you" and "Questions?" slides.

WHEN IT'S A TEAM GAME

In a follow-up discussion with your CEO about "Industry 2020," she brings up the possibility of you delivering the keynote speech with some other members of the senior management team.

Ultimately, Peggy decides this conference won't be the best setting for a team event, but she makes it clear that she wants you to organize and participate in such an initiative in the near future. She recognizes the potential of a multi-person opportunity, and, as you know, wants to showcase her group's talent as part of a strategy to raise the company's profile.

You're not so enthusiastic about the "team" part. You know that while speaking on your own can be challenging, speaking as a member of a group can be downright daunting.

No argument there. However, you'd better get used to the idea of presenting with your colleagues. With the growing emphasis on teamwork in business, more and more employees are being called upon to speak alongside their co-workers, internally and externally.

Certainly, there are plenty of risks. Too often, team presentations succumb to the inherent difficulty of assimilating multiple personalities, styles, and priorities, and crumple into disjointed, ineffectual dog-and-pony shows.

However, when a team is clicking on all cylinders, there are few communication initiatives more forceful. Whether the collective goal is to share a vision, recommend a course of action, or win a piece of business, cohesion is the key to success.

Here's how to make the principles of great teamwork successful at the lectern.

Pick a leader

There's no way around it: someone needs to have overall responsibility for your group presentation.

When you're deciding on a leader, aim high. The more elevated the chief organizer's rank, the more profile and resources your project will be given.

For your first team event, I'd go for Peggy herself. Why not? The worst she can say is no, and she'll be flattered that you asked. If she does agree to come on board, you know you'll have the weight of the CEO behind you.

The leader doesn't necessarily have to participate in the presentation, but ultimately makes the final decision on content, and on who speaks and in what order.

Ideally, though, the leader takes part in the production itself, kicking it off, introducing fellow speakers, setting the context, and then, once the others have completed their sections, wrapping up the collective story with a commanding summarization and call to action.

Keep it simple

Use the classic, tried-and-true Power of Three to organize your presentation under the sections Introduction, Body and Conclusion.

The most senior speaker almost always handles the introduction and conclusion, providing a nice sense of symmetry, organization, and authority.

Three presenters can participate in the delivery of the body, each covering a main point or category. That means a maximum of four speakers for your group presentation; there are precious few exceptions.

The more presenters, the less impact they deliver, and the greater the chances of foul-ups and misunderstandings.

Play to your strengths

Increase your team's prospects of success by giving the more skilled, confident speakers additional presentation time, but not so much that lesser lights are marginalized.

Protect weaker presenters (and enhance listeners' perception of their routine) by having them introduce an interesting clip, an attention-grabbing prop, or an especially well-crafted PowerPoint slide. Give them the outstanding stuff to refer to and you'll raise their confidence and their game.

Of course individual egos must kneel in service to the greater good. That applies to even a team's most senior speaker, who, as it may turn out, can't make the oratorical grade. In such a case, the top dog's time needs to be chopped, making for a shorter introduction and conclusion.

Sometimes, that's not such a bad thing.

Look and act like a team

You may dislike a particular co-presenter, but in the image-based universe of team productions, you have to appear as though you vacation together.

That means relating as if you were trusted colleagues — with copious amounts of eye contact, frequent use of first names, and full-on listening techniques. Audiences can quickly perceive dissension, however slight, within a team in presentation mode. Nothing can undermine a group's credibility faster than a harsh word, or even a cross look, from one colleague to another.

Your listeners will ask, "If they can't even give a presentation together, how could they possibly work on our business together?"

It's a reasonable question. You're in it together, as a team. So look and act like it.

Rehearse your transitions

The final key to a successful team presentation lies in the transition, or "hand-off," between speakers. Just as the baton in a relay race requires a smooth, sure transfer from one runner to another, so the story in a group narrative needs to be advanced.

Rehearsal takes on even greater significance in a group project. The effective linking of content involves a kind of verbal choreography that comes about only when each presenter has a thorough knowledge of the subject matter covered by the other speakers — especially his or her closing paragraphs — and then builds seamlessly on it.

This smooth transitioning takes co-operation and a great deal of practice.

All the presenters should consider themselves understudies and learn the script of at least one other speaker cold; it's a coordinated strategy that, in effect, backs up the entire presentation. You need to be able to cover for each other, if something goes wrong.

It's what teammates do.

Seven Steps to a Great Team Presentation

1. Pick a leader.
2. Keep it simple — the most senior speaker handles the introduction and conclusion, the three others a main body point each.
3. Give better speakers slightly more presentation time.
4. "Protect" weaker presenters with great content.
5. Look — and act — like trusted colleagues.
6. Learn at least one other script.
7. Rehearse your transitions.

THE DRILL ON PANELS

The organizers of "Industry 2020" have called.

Your presentation will take place on Monday, the first day of the three-day conference. They've also requested your presence on Wednesday, to participate in a panel discussion of prominent figures in your field.

Yikes! Are you supposed to vacuum after the conference as well?

Be cool. Panel discussions represent another forum in which to speak like a leader. You have to be careful, though. Panels can be tricky. They've earned their uneven reputation.

That's because they're often ponderous, unfocused affairs that drone self-consciously on as trapped, distressed audience members pray for an early wrap. It almost never happens. In fact, panels habitually run over their time due to poor planning and weak moderators.

The potential of panels

When they're run right, however, panel discussions can dazzle and inform.

When a group of astute, motivated participants brings differing perspectives to a significant, well-defined issue while respecting each other (and the concept of time), listeners benefit from the rich discourse.

Like preparing and delivering a great speech, it takes a lot of work to get there. In fact, organizing and facilitating an outstanding panel can qualify as a more complex task than nailing a first-rate presentation, given the unpredictability of a conversation involving multiple players, and the inclination of some to amble off on self-indulgent musings and tangents.

To work at its best, a panel discussion has to be operated like a boot camp, while appearing to onlookers like a summer camp: inclusive, stimulating, and warm.

But that's at its best.

Most panels don't achieve anywhere near that level, underachieving in a stilted, self-conscious way that leads a host of notables in the business and artistic worlds to politely take a pass on them.

It's become hip to inform one's peers, "I don't do panels."

Politicians have no choice, though. They're obligated to take part. Few of them ever look happy or comfortable doing so.

Clearly, panels need help. There are ways to reach the communication potential of these maligned group discussions in three key areas: planning, moderating, and participating.

Planning

The main advantage of a panel over a speech is that it will provide, or should, several points of view on a subject. Frequently, though, organizers will invite a coterie of lumpy, risk-averse company lifers (not you, of course) to participate; individuals who view a matter through the same slender prism. Listeners, meanwhile, can be rendered comatose.

When planning a panel yourself, ask, "What combination of guests will provide the audience with the best informational and entertainment value?"

Seek out subject matter and industry experts who'll

bring with them new perspectives, insights, and theories, speakers who'll have the moxie to render definitive, even contentious statements and stick by them. Look for participants who'll pack an edge.

You don't want a free-for-all, but you do want ardent discussion and debate.

With the credentials of your speakers established, mix them up according to experience, age, gender, and industry profile. Build your panel with imagination and balance, always sifting the suitability of candidates through your primary filter: the interests of the audience.

Try and limit the number of panelists to four. At five, the conversation tends to become scattered. It also becomes increasingly difficult to ensure that everyone gets equal time. Limit discussions to an hour, ninety minutes at an absolute maximum.

Moderating

To run a panel effectively, you need to take charge from the outset, without having participants and listeners resent you for it.

Demonstrate any sign of ego or impatience and it will work against you. Consider yourself an affable, skilled host who directs formless conversations to positive, even rousing resolution, and tactfully but firmly informs guests when they've overstayed their welcome.

Open the proceedings by welcoming the audience, introducing yourself, and briefly reviewing the topic for discussion. You could then say, "Before I introduce the members of our panel, I'd like to explain how we'll spend our hour together. First, each panelist will make a brief opening statement. [Bring out the hook for each speaker at three minutes.] Then they'll engage in what we anticipate will be a spirited discussion for thirty minutes. Finally, they'll take your questions. We'll adjourn the session at 4:00 p.m. Now, let's get to it!"

Moderators set the tone and the parameters.

They need to keep all of the panel members involved, contributing, and speaking to the topic at hand. (Sample moderator comment: "That's a great insight, Mr. Smith. You bring a valuable perspective to this issue. On the wider question, though, let's ask Ms. Collins to expand upon the view she expressed a few minutes ago.")

Participating

As a panelist, success means cutting through the cacophony to tell your story with clarity.

Use the old reliable Power of Three to build a strong foundation with your opening statement, which needs to include your position on the subject of discussion, and your main points.

Having laid down your template at the outset, you

can return to it continuously, building on your points and supporting them with examples, statistics, and references.

A sound, well-organized story generates confidence and influence. When other panelists challenge you, you can simply employ a range of transition or bridging phrases to neutralize their impertinence and return smoothly to your narrative.

For example: "I'm surprised to hear that, Bill. My experience has been just the opposite." Or even, "Karen, clearly we see things differently. My position is this."

But you need to say it all respectfully.

The audience will be watching closely to see how the participants get along. You want to be friendly and accommodating, interacting with your colleagues as if you're the most charming person on earth (channel George Clooney).

Use the panelists' first names, and compliment them genuinely, if you're impressed by their commentary.

If there's discord, agree to disagree. Aim to leave the proceedings on a high. It's the moderator's job to generate that kind of outcome, but in my experience few do it well. If there's a lack of direction from the moderator, step up and provide it.

Wrap up your mini-presentation with a robust conclusion, perhaps even a provocative prediction. That will get everyone's attention.

Seven Steps to Panel Perfection

1. Have a tight, well-integrated story.
2. Provide meaningful examples, observations, and insights.
3. Keep your remarks focused and short.
4. Treat your fellow panelists with courtesy and respect.
5. Use transitions to bridge back to your story.
6. Agree to disagree.
7. End with impact.

LOCKED AND LOADED

Time goes by in a hurry.

"Industry 2020" is a mere week away. You feel ready.

You've gone through several full-blown rehearsals with your CEO and her team. Peggy and her crew like what they saw, especially your last run-through, two days ago.

The comprehensive process of preparation you've undertaken with Peggy has definitely strengthened your relationship with her. Others have noticed. Even Tim, soon to leave for Germany, seems to regard you with enhanced respect.

At Peggy's suggestion, you've done what all smart executives do when preparing for a major presentation: you've made a video of yourself rehearsing.

The fastest way to get better

Seeing yourself as others do can be a humbling experience. Few people enjoy watching themselves speak.

Many presenters get fixated on issues of physical appearance, with the perception of burgeoning weight and receding hairlines as their primary obsessions.

They should instead be honing in on the more objective picture and asking, "How am I communicating? Is my story clear? Am I speaking with the best interest of the audience at heart?"

By watching yourself, you can identify and, as a result, reduce or eliminate the verbal and physical components that distract an audience and prevent a stellar performance.

Is your narrative marked by "ahs" and "ums"?

Do you rock back and forth?

Run your fingers through your hair?

Whatever you say, and however you say it, you can improve it. Great communicators speak *cleanly.* There's nothing in their language, verbal or body, to take away from their message.

How do you get to the point where you're presenting cleanly? By speaking, watching recordings of yourself, and soliciting and accepting as many presentation opportunities as reasonably possible, in all manner of circumstances.

You'll get better by taking risks and occasionally falling short. That's life.

You've prepared extensively for "Industry 2020." You know your story and you've constructed it well.

The introduction, to be delivered against the backdrop of your company's logo, runs five minutes. The body, organized under three main categories — products, partnerships, and people — features just twelve PowerPoint slides. It's been timed to sixteen minutes.

You've decided, as part of the body of your speech, to show a seventy-five-second video clip (the length of a television news story) featuring interviews with three customers, real people.

Nicely done.

The conclusion, with the company logo returning to the screen, will be delivered over four minutes.

You've choreographed your script, underlining key lines for emphasis and reminding yourself to pause, stop, and even smile.

You're locked and loaded. You're ready to go. You're prepared.

But are you really?

Preparing for — whatever

Preparation is more than simply knowing your narrative and your audience. It means being psychologically ready for virtually any occurrence, from an opening challenge conveyed by an irate listener, to speaking time that's cut short, to technology that blows up.

Leaders respond to such circumstances with self-assurance and poise, without even a hint of irritation.

They know that observers will form an immediate opinion of them, based on their reaction to misfortune. They also know that in many ways, a presentation is much like a relationship: you gain or lose the most respect in the tough times, not the good times.

I almost feel badly revisiting the following story, because it adds insult to injury, and because I've made my share of presenting mistakes (and then some).

So I'll allay my conscience by sharing two stories, one about Jeanine Pirro and one about me.

It was August 2005. Jeanine Pirro was officially declaring her candidacy for the New York Senate seat held by Hillary Clinton, when she stumbled badly.

"Hillary Clinton," she said, then abruptly stopped. "I'm sorry," Ms. Pirro muttered, searching through her notes as onlookers shifted uncomfortably and television cameras recorded every mute, excruciating moment.

"Do you have page ten," Ms. Pirro asked her staff in a voice that everyone present could easily hear. "Who's got…?"

After what seemed like a year — it was actually thirty-two seconds — she resumed her formal remarks.

It was a rocky start to a campaign that just got worse, and Ms. Pirro eventually withdrew from the race. Certainly, this oratorical gaffe wasn't solely responsible for the demise of her Senate aspirations, but it did communicate three powerful, negative messages: she was disorganized, easily flustered, and incapable of speaking about her opponent without a script.

The three-ring binder, a simple office supply, easily qualifies as one of the great inventions in the history of communication. It could have saved Ms. Pirro the calamity of a missing speech page.

For your presentations, three-hole punch a copy of your PowerPoint deck or script and place it in a binder in your favourite colour. (I'm superstitious that way.)

Take the binder with you to the lectern. You'll look organized and professional, and you'll never get caught out. Be prepared to present seamlessly off the hard copy if your technology implodes.

How *not* to speak like a leader

I was feeling pretty confident when I ambled to the front of the room on a Western road trip to address a group of twenty investment advisors on the subject of "How Leaders Speak."

The client company had been very good to me, and I wanted to do well, as we all do, all of the time.

I had dutifully arrived at the seminar early to test my technology, a trusty laptop featuring my digital clips. It had come through without a hitch at least a couple of hundred times before. All was well. The hotel projector played the clips with no problem.

Life was good.

There was a short break before I was to speak, and I had plugged in my computer. The resulting images appeared greenish on the screen, so my client suggested that I turn off my laptop and fire it up again to get a clearer, better definition.

I did. And the images never appeared again.

The projector, for whatever reason, wasn't reading my laptop, and the investment advisors had already begun filing back into the room.

Not good.

My client, ever the professional, managed to transfer some (but not all) of my clips to a memory stick and play them off her laptop, which, thankfully, the projector was still reading.

However, I felt the impact of my presentation had dissipated and I struggled during the next forty minutes. I was off balance and angry with myself.

I could have avoided all the drama by bringing along my own memory stick, with all my clips duly categorized. I did have a DVD backup of the clips that my videographer had prepared for me, but I'd been distracted by a work issue before hurriedly leaving on the road trip and had forgotten to bring it with me.

Lesson re-learned. Institute travel checklist.

Have a comprehensive checklist and go over it carefully before leaving for "Industry 2020" and Las Vegas. Because when it comes to speaking like a leader, the preparation never really ends.

Ten Items for Your Presentation Checklist

1. The date, time, and location of your speaking event, as well as detailed directions to the venue.
2. The name, telephone numbers, and email address of your main contact, along with those of his or her backup.
3. The location and time of your rehearsal, along with the contact information for your audiovisual support person.
4. Confirmation that your presentation has been emailed and received in good order by the event organizers, and has been tested on their computers to ensure it opens and runs properly.
5. A copy of the presentation on your laptop, and on a memory stick.
6. An adapter, power cord, and spare battery for your laptop.
7. A hard copy of the presentation in a three-ring binder.
8. Children's Gravol® antacids, and aspirin.
9. A humorous video clip that you can instruct your A/V person to play if you run into a rough patch during the presentation and need to lighten the proceedings.
10. A copy of *How Leaders Speak*, preferably autographed.

The Second Key — Certainty

You've just arrived in Las Vegas.

It's Sunday, the day before your big presentation at "Industry 2020," and you're starting to feel apprehensive.

You want so badly to speak like a leader tomorrow. You want to speak with certainty. However, you're feeling far from certain right now — you're feeling nervous.

That's natural. It's an indication that you're committed to doing well, and that you have respect for the people who'll show up to hear you tomorrow. Those are good things.

PRE-PRESENTATION JITTERS

Public speaking remains among humankind's greatest, and most irrational, fears. The anxiety stems from a kind of self-absorption. We become overly concerned with our act, our routine, and how listeners will judge it — and us.

The antidote is simple. We have to take the attention off ourselves and direct it to where it belongs, on the audience.

The best speakers know that. They also know that a single presentation, however significant, is rarely critical to the survival of democracy.

Accomplished presenters know that while speaking effectively can quickly affect one's career trajectory, for the most part they'll be evaluated according to how well they communicate over time. It's cumulative.

Perspective is key here.

No one speaks like a leader right out of the box. It takes commitment, patience, and the realization that, on occasion, we'll falter.

Big deal.

It's been said that fear is a bully, and if you don't take it on, early and often, it can destroy the wonderful experience of addressing others.

The fear factor

I once conducted a presentation skills session with a middle-aged executive who'd long been terrified of public speaking. In fact, he'd delivered his high school valedictory address with his back to the audience.

What would his classmates have remembered all these years, his words or his posterior? The story doesn't end there, though. This executive eventually confronted his presentation anxieties and now speaks, as a leader in his field, facing his listeners.

I also worked with a highly successful television producer who was so intimidated by the prospect of embarking on a cross-country speaking tour that he could barely function. I decided to play amateur psychiatrist.

"What's the worst thing that could happen?" I asked.

"I'd freeze and go blank," he replied.

"Then what would happen?" I inquired.

"The audience would get uncomfortable; some people would laugh."

"Okay," I responded. "What would you do then?"

"I'd probably freak out," he said.

We constructed an absurd scenario in which the producer's pants fell down, he tripped running off the stage, was loudly ridiculed by the audience, and was deeply humiliated.

And so it went. You get the picture.

Even in this terrible fantasy, when he got up the next day, the sun had risen in the sky, his wife and children still loved him, and he remained a successful television producer who makes more in a year than I will in several lifetimes.

There's reality, and then there's your mind. When it comes to public speaking, keep your mind rooted in reality.

Starting your presentation the day before

Today, Sunday, your mind should be happy and relaxed, but not inactive.

There are several steps you can take to help ensure that you serve your audience well tomorrow. You've already nailed the first one: you arrived in Vegas early.

I always like to get into the city in which I'm speaking as early as possible the day before an engagement. It enables you to acclimatize to a new location and time zone, read the local papers, and go for a relaxing, rejuvenating walk or run.

Your presentation really should start the day before your allotted speaking time.

When you pick up your speaker's credentials at the conference registration table, introduce yourself to organizers and delegates. Start making the friends and supporters you'll need tomorrow.

Ideally, you'll want to have arranged a run-through of your presentation in the hall or room where it will take place. A full-on rehearsal can eliminate a litany of problems and surprises on Monday.

Make friends and influence people

Test your technology thoroughly and bond with the audio-visual personnel. You definitely want these good people onside. They're experts in their field, and aren't always afforded the attention and respect they deserve.

They also have the ability to make you look very good, or very bad. Learn their first names — and use those names frequently in conversation ("Buddy" just won't cut it).

If you're unable to rehearse, at the very least check out the room in which you'll be speaking. Why? We're creatures of habit. We fear the unknown and luxuriate in the familiar. You'll appreciate the pre-emptive visit when you stride to the lectern for real, in front of five hundred onlookers.

Your brain will say, "Hey, we've been here before. This isn't so bad. We can relax a bit now!"

You've done your preparation. You know your story. And tomorrow, you're going to implement another step that will empower you to speak with certainty: you're going to take your time.

You're going to start and finish slowly, like a leader.

Eat and drink lightly tonight. The last thing you want tomorrow is to be suffering from indigestion or, worse, a hangover.

You're all set to head up to your room to review your presentation notes when a work colleague calls you on your cellphone. He wants you to join a group that's heading out to the casinos. It's a major party opportunity.

"Come with us," he says.

But you know the answer to that, my friend. The answer is, "No, thank you."

You have a big day tomorrow. You're speaking at "Industry 2020."

THE BEAUTY OF SLOW

The research indicates that we make up our minds about someone new in a hurry, ninety seconds to be exact. Think about it. Your listeners are going to form an opinion about you in a minute and a half.

Maximize the odds that they'll like and respect you. Start by speaking slowly.

At the outset of a presentation by an unknown or little-known speaker, audiences are generally uncertain about how the interaction will unfold. While everyone wants the communication to succeed, a low-grade anxiety nevertheless permeates, an unspoken fear that the presenter will tank, and that listeners will have to endure seemingly endless minutes of awkward or even painful discourse.

By starting slowly, speakers help themselves and the audience by easing the ambient tension and engaging their listeners as if they were a group of trusted friends. And friends don't rush each other.

A slow, purposeful, well-crafted opening tells those in attendance that a speaker is thoughtful, confident, and respectful of their relationship. A rushed introduction indicates the opposite — that a presenter is scattered, insecure, and either intimidated, or dismissive.

Most executives speak far too quickly in the first few critical minutes of a talk, and only begin to slow down as their nerves settle. Leaders do the reverse. They start slowly and then speed up when their content requires it.

The presidential pace

U.S. President Barack Obama has raised the technique of commencing a speech slowly to an art.

On September 9, 2009, in an address to a Joint Session of Congress on Health Care, the President took a minute and thirty-five seconds — with applause — to deliver these opening words.

> Madam Speaker, Vice President Biden, members of Congress, and the American people.
>
> When I spoke here last winter, this nation was facing the worst economic crisis since the Great Depression. We were losing an average of seven hundred thousand jobs per month. Credit was frozen. And our financial system was on the verge of collapse.
>
> As any American who is still looking for work or a way to pay their bills will tell you, we are by no means out of the woods. A full and

vibrant recovery is still many months away. And I will not let up until those Americans who seek jobs can find them — until those businesses that seek capital and credit can thrive; until all responsible homeowners can stay in their homes. That is our ultimate goal. But thanks to the bold and decisive action we've taken since January, I can stand here with confidence and say that we have pulled this economy back from the brink.

Most people speak at between 120 and 170 words a minute. Mr. Obama delivered those words on health care at the rate of 125 words a minute.

In fact, on the night of his dramatic win in the Iowa Democratic Primary on January 3, 2008, Mr. Obama took a full seventy-nine seconds — an eternity in current-day oratory — to deliver his opening.

It was politics as theatre, and Mr. Obama played his role to perfection, never rushing his lines, and frequently pausing to let his audience cheer. Before commencing his remarks, he said "Thank you" at least ten times over the applause of his listeners.

Then he began:

Thank you, Iowa. You know, they said — they said, they said — this day would never come. They said our sights were set too high. They said this country was too divided; too disillusioned to ever come together around a common purpose. But on this January night — at this defining moment in history — you have done what the cynics said we couldn't do. You have done what the State of New Hampshire can do in five days. You have done what America can do in this New Year, 2008.

Of course, Mr. Obama had to stop and wait three times for the crowd's cheering to subside. Chances are that you won't be interrupted by cheers. Your pauses will have power nonetheless, providing your audience with an opportunity to reflect upon what you've just said.

Accomplished speakers like Mr. Obama know that when you start slowly, a host of great things happen.

You impress your listeners with the fact that you're calm and relaxed under pressure, which leads to a connection based on credibility rather than anxiety.

You think more clearly and logically, without the mental stress brought about by rapid-fire rhetoric.

You're less likely to flub words and phrases, which boosts your confidence as you deliver your remarks smoothly.

Finally, you just look smarter, more considered. In the hurly-burly of fast, ill-considered chatter, you stand out.

Leaders have recognized and implemented the power of speaking slowly for a long time.

A general's story

On April 19, 1951, U.S. General Douglas MacArthur gave what is widely considered to be one of the finest speeches of the twentieth century.

It was a farewell address, delivered to Congress to mark the end of MacArthur's long Army career after he was relieved of his command in the Far East by President Harry Truman. The two had disagreed over military strategy in the ongoing Korean War.

MacArthur's speech was mesmerizing, beautifully constructed, passionately delivered, and slow. As he prepared to deliver his final words, there was a long, emotional pause.

Then came these timeless words:

> I am closing my fifty-two years of military service. When I joined the Army, even before the turn of the century, it was the fulfillment of all my boyish hopes and dreams. The world has turned over many times since I took the oath on the plain at West Point, and the hopes and dreams have long since vanished. But I still remember the refrain of one of the most popular barrack ballads of that day, which proclaimed most proudly that "Old Soldiers Never Die, They Just Fade Away." And like the old soldier of that ballad, I now close my military career and just fade away — an old soldier who tried to do his duty as God gave him the light to see that duty. Goodbye.

It took MacArthur more than a minute and a half to deliver that passage (although several seconds were taken up waiting for the audience's applause to quiet). Most speakers today would rattle off the section in half the time, lessening the impact of their narrative and conclusion.

I've been a presentation skills coach for a long time, and each day I become more convinced of the power of speaking slowly.

It's essential to go slowly at the start of a presentation, as well as in places that require special emphasis throughout the body, and in the conclusion, where themes are summarized. The slower and more emphatic the delivery here, the more a speaker's final words will resonate with the audience.

If you aspire to speak like a leader, bookend the first and last minutes of your script with a delivery that has less speed and more drama. And mark up your notes with reminders to do what great speakers from every generation have done.

They've gone slowly.

THE BIG DAY

Good morning. It's presentation day!

I have a personal coach who has helped me enormously with her business advice since 2002.

Often, before a speaking engagement, I'll call her

for some last-minute counsel. She always says the same thing, "Make it about *them.*"

Make it about your listeners. That's your theme for today, and for every day in which you have the privilege of addressing others.

It's 7:00 a.m., and you're speaking at 11:00. A pretty good slot. Not as good as first thing in the morning, which is a great time to speak, but better than mid-afternoon, when delegates can be fading and restless. Ironically the final position of the day can be an advantageous one, giving energetic presenters the chance to make a big impression if they stay within their time; crowds frequently rally for the last speaker.

Whenever you're scheduled, you have to make the best of it.

Be careful what you consume

Have a light breakfast. If I have a morning presentation I'll have scrambled eggs, but no toast. Bread crumbs can stick in your teeth.

Once, before an afternoon webinar, I made the mistake of eating potato chips at lunch. I was frantically digging chips out of the spaces between my teeth right up until showtime.

Like I said: I've made every mistake in the book.

Go easy on the caffeine. I allow myself one coffee at breakfast. After that, I drink plenty of room temperature water. Avoid milk and yogurt before you speak; dairy products create mucus and can lead to irritating throat-clearing.

If my stomach is upset the morning of a presentation, I'll take a couple of children's Gravol (the adult version can make you groggy) with a shot or two of cola.

I know, it sounds weird, but it works for me.

It's now 8:30 a.m. and you've arrived at the conference.

In effect, you're already on.

It amazes me that so many speakers ignore the very people they'll soon have to count on for attention and support. Don't wait for an invitation; introduce yourself around and reacquaint yourself with old colleagues.

Smile. Broadly.

Act in every way like you're delighted to be there, and you'll soon begin to feel like it. Besides, it's too late to bolt now. Your CEO has just arrived.

Peggy looks nervous for you, or maybe her demeanour has nothing to do with you. It doesn't matter.

You've determined that however this presentation goes down, you're going to be yourself.

It pays to be "you"

There's remarkable power in being "you." It's who everyone is expecting, so don't let someone else show up in your place. If you do try to take on another persona, a puffed-up or too-humble version of yourself, listeners will sense your insincerity and tune you out.

Audiences for the most part are tremendously supportive, especially when they perceive that speakers are being true to themselves. So be you, imperfections and all. Chances are that no one listening will be perfect, either.

Once, I conducted a communications skills workshop with a group of intellectually challenged adults. They were terrific presenters — they were themselves. One animated young woman, upon receiving the videotape of her speech at the end of the session, hugged it and exclaimed, "I love me!"

You do the same. Love you.

Finally, forget about delivering a perfect presentation. If your goal is to be perfect and you flub a line early, a little voice in your head will helpfully inform you that you've failed. I've seen speakers go right down the chute after that.

Aim for excellence instead.

All of us will stumble, because we're human. However, if you serve the needs of your audience with discipline and enthusiasm, few will remember that you were less than perfect. Or even care.

TAKING ON THE TOUGH STUFF

Certainty in a presentation means confidence in yourself, in your story, and in your ability to take on any situation, however difficult.

The chances of anything going awry at "Industry 2020" are remote, but you have to be ready all the same. Here's an example of why:

When the crackling smart vice-president of a financial services company delivered a speech at an important conference, his remarks seemed off. At first, the executive couldn't figure out why his address didn't get the traction it needed, or the response he felt it deserved.

But during an in-depth postmortem, he was able to figure it out. An issue that had developed before he'd even begun to speak was the cause. Because he didn't deal with the concern from the outset — or, in the lexicon of a certain communication skills coach, "kill it dead" — the problem grew, eventually overpowering the presenter and his presentation.

Deal with difficulty directly

Whatever the interaction, a speech, a meeting, or a media interview, impediments to understanding have to be eliminated at the start, or they'll have turned nasty by the end. You need to take them on.

As happens all too frequently at speaking events, the vice-president had been poorly introduced. Before the event, he had sent a lengthy biography to conference organizers and promptly forgot all about it. After all, he was mostly concerned with his presentation.

However, in relinquishing control of his own introduction, he left it up to the moderator to shape the words that would form the audience's early perception of him. And the moderator went over the top, observing that the young executive had virtually transformed his organization.

He hadn't.

Listening to the introduction, the vice-president was rendered nearly apoplectic. As the remarks concluded, he smiled wanly. Shaken by the erroneous buildup, he sensed audience skepticism and perhaps even resentment. He stepped to the lectern with a decision to make. Should he correct the record?

"Too complicated," he thought.

He soldiered on, distracted and tentative for his entire address.

Unresolved issues get in the way

Those in attendance sensed something was askew. A strange group psychology takes over in such circumstances; the members of the audience bend, virtually in unison, to the negative ambience. At this point, the likelihood that a speaker will connect with the crowd becomes almost non-existent.

With a little forethought, it all could have been avoided. The executive could have written a brief, buoyant introduction that accurately summarized his career accomplishments and sent it to the conference organizers with a note that read, "This is how I'm typically introduced."

He'll definitely do that next time.

When inaccurate or misleading information gets dispensed, all remaining narrative staggers under its pressing, expanding weight. You can see this phenomenon play out in the media. When, during interviews, business and political types don't have the experience or mettle to correct what they believe to be false or biased material, they find themselves in distress.

They soon discover that the failure to challenge statements or questions featuring faulty intelligence or skewed attitudes constitutes tacit validation of them.

Addressing the "wimp factor"

A classic example of a public figure aggressively tackling a negative stereotype occurred in the late 1980s, when then U.S. Vice-President George Herbert Walker Bush was forced to confront growing media and public sentiment that he was an ineffectual lackey to President Ronald Reagan.

It was called the "wimp factor."

In a famous *60 Minutes* television interview with Diane Sawyer, Mr. Bush struck back.

I'll put my record out there with anybody. You know that I was shot down two months after my twentieth birthday, fighting for my country? I didn't detect any wimp factor there. Do you know we had to sit, my wife and I, and watch a child wrenched from our hearts in six months of cancer, knowing she was going to die? A little strength comes from that. Do you know that I've run agencies like the CIA and restored the morale out there by making tough decisions, moving people around, not jumping out trying to get credit. But if his [columnist George Will's] complaint is that I'm loyal to this president — guilty as charged.

Invariably, the facts we require to respond to a tough question — or salvage a bad introduction — are contained in our personal story. To communicate like a leader, you need to quickly retrieve the appropriate material and deploy it adroitly.

The financial services vice-president who was poorly introduced would have done well to set the record straight by correcting the faulty information, without criticizing the moderator. That would have been ungracious — and problematic. The audience might have sympathized with the moderator, and turned against the speaker.

Instead, he might have said, "Thank you for those kind words. I should clarify one point — while I'd certainly like to take credit for transforming the company, I can only take credit for the marketing division. The company is next!"

Take on the tough stuff early, and it will always go better for you in the end.

AN HOUR TO LIFTOFF

It's now 10:00 a.m. — an hour until your presentation.

You may find yourself sitting at a table with a group of conference officials and speakers, near the stage. Take an interest in the proceedings. Be engaged. It's professional courtesy to encourage other presenters, to pay full attention as they speak, nodding, smiling and applauding when appropriate.

You'll appreciate that level of support when you take the lectern.

Communicate like a leader as you wait your turn to speak, without saying a word. Look calm, confident, and composed.

At this point it's really too late to be studying your presentation, all spiffy in its blue, three-ring binder. At this point you either know it, or you don't. Besides, staring at your script now would be rude and inconsiderate.

At conferences, I'm baffled by speakers who, before a big speech, will ignore everyone around them to review their notes, self-involved and frowning. Then, when it's their turn to talk, they'll expect the crowd to love them unconditionally.

But you don't operate like that.

As you wait your turn to speak, rehearse the opening in your mind.

Take more time with each run-through; it's almost impossible to speak too slowly.

Smile, now, while you wait, when you're being introduced, and as you begin to address the audience.

The longest hour? It all depends on you

The hour before a presentation has the potential to be the longest sixty minutes in life, if you make it about you. But don't make it about you, make it about your listeners. Think about how you're going to serve them, and how positive an experience that will be for everyone.

Of course, you can't invest a great deal of emotional capital in the prospect that the audience will instantly be into you, or even pay a great deal of attention to you.

You're not owed rapt attention. You have to earn it, through preparation and certainty.

With the pace of life these days and all that's going on in the world, listeners are more distracted than ever.

A speaker at a conference in Washington, D.C. found that out in September 2008, shortly after Lehman Brothers had gone under.

He was doing his best, but his listeners just weren't responding. They were busy contemplating the deepening financial crisis and their own shrinking portfolios.

Many were doing more than just thinking about it all. With their BlackBerrys and other personal digital assistants, they were checking on the roiling markets in real time.

There's nothing like a global financial meltdown to get the heads of your audience members bowed before their PDAs, all but ignoring the keen, well-prepared presenter before them.

Welcome to the age of distraction.

Long before the financial chaos of 2008, speakers were complaining that it's becoming harder to overcome listeners' obsession with technology and induce them to focus.

And it's not just current events that are responsible — whether it's to keep in touch with the office or check in with family and friends, audience members are increasingly using their PDAs to multitask. Anywhere. Any time.

So how, as a speaker, do you compete?

How do you communicate in a way that compels the members of the crowd to shut down — or at least holster — their handheld gadgetry and actually listen?

Following some key principles will help you make the connection.

Speak when they're ready

Address your listeners (whether it's two or two hundred) only when they're prepared to hear you.

If you're about to speak and a substantial segment of the audience is talking, reading, or texting, say in a strong, firm, friendly voice, "Good morning" or "Good afternoon."

Then don't say a word.

Just stand at the lectern or at your meeting chair, making eye contact with the most obvious offenders.

Don't smile, don't frown, and don't reveal even a trace of irritation or impatience. Just wait.

You're sending an authoritative message — that you're no patsy, and that you intend to be treated with courtesy. Eventually (and it's bound to feel like an eternity), the audience will go quiet and regard you with a combination of respect and curiosity.

Now you're ready to do your thing.

Go easy on the ground rules

Most people now consider it their constitutional right to check their PDAs at any venue, at any time and under any circumstance. Little can be done to stop them.

Indeed, I once attended a presentation where the officious host of the event commanded more than three hundred attendees to turn off their BlackBerrys.

No one did, at least no one that I could see, but everyone resented him for the order.

"What?" You could almost hear the audience respond in unison. "Who do you think you are?"

If possible, try to avoid telling people what to do.

You can only do that if they're working for you, and some organizations have banned the use of handheld devices during internal meetings. But if you're speaking outside the office, accept the fact that you'll have far less control.

In such situations, it's best to have the master of ceremonies or organizer explain the rules of engagement as part of "housekeeping" duties.

It's really not your job. More importantly, as a presenter, it's far more difficult to forge a motivational connection with listeners after you've said, "Please remember to set your cellphones and BlackBerrys on vibrate."

It's commonplace, near-remedial language, and difficult for the crowd to leave behind as you attempt to open your formal remarks with impact. Besides, some audience members may take offence at the inference that they're not responsible enough to have already taken care of the vibrate option.

Keep your cool

There's nothing more irritating than being interrupted mid-sentence by one of those cloying 1980s pop-music ring tones from a cellphone. (A warning: violence is never an option. You can be excused, though, for fantasizing about ripping the infuriating apparatus out of the clutched hands of a near-hypnotized listener as you deliver your killer presentation.)

Aggravations can also take the form of a sound system that crackles, an incessantly coughing audience member, or a laptop that takes forever to play your digital clips.

It's life.

The key point is that you need to accept such occurrences with an almost Zen-like calm, good humour, and patience. If you make a big deal of them, they'll stick in the collective consciousness of the audience and you'll come off looking like an angry victim, not a composed leader.

Listeners will remember the intensity of your response, not the quality of your talk.

Use your judgment

Occasionally, a distraction can be too egregious to ignore.

If, in a small group meeting, a participant is chatting on a cellphone loudly enough for others to hear, the skilled presenter will stop speaking, look patiently at the discourteous party, and wait.

Almost always, the offender will sheepishly end the conversation and return to the fold. Rarely, the intrusion continues. When it does, and if it's serious enough, it's time to lower the verbal boom.

"Excuse me," the speaker might say, without smiling, "would you please take your conversation outside?"

With a crowd of considerable size, though, you'd never call out the offender in the far corner of the room, rapping on his cell. That would be too disruptive and unsettling to the majority. In times like that, let it go.

Sometimes you'll get lucky and audience members will self-regulate inappropriate cellphone use. But don't count on it.

Ultimately, the more interesting you are, the more likely it is that those in attendance will actually pay attention to what you have to say.

Listeners, being human, will at least occasionally give in to their compulsion and check their PDAs. That's when you have to demonstrate a little compassion.

THOSE FIRST NINETY SECONDS

It's 11:05 a.m.

You should be on stage by now, weaving your magic, but the conference is running late, as conferences tend to do.

Be cool. Here's where we separate the pros from the amateurs.

The previous speaker is just wrapping up, and you'll soon be introduced. There's a tendency at this point to become overwhelmed by all you have to do and want to achieve — deliver a sharp, spellbinding presentation to a critical crowd of thought leaders, and then manage a question-and-answer session with cleverness and dexterity.

Take the pressure off yourself. Aim to succeed in small increments of time.

For starters, aim to connect in those first ninety seconds.

Within the first ninety seconds, a job interviewer will be impressed by a candidate, or dismiss him from contention; a prospect will respond to a sales representative, or start issuing signals for her to hurry up and get lost.

An audience will bond with a speaker — or not.

What would you think of you?

You have a minute and a half to forge a connection. Curiously, we often fail to pay enough attention to those vital early moments, going forward as if everyone already knows, loves, and respects us. "Hey, it's me. I'm great. Now, let me tell you more about me."

Put yourself in the place of a listener. What would you think of you? That's a legitimate question as you gear up for your big presentation.

Humans have been making lightning-quick judgments about each other for thousands of years. It's been a matter of instinct — and survival. If you hesitated too long before determining that the hirsute figure looming in front of you was a member of the enemy tribe, you'd be quickly dispatched.

As a result, we as a species have tended to err on the

side of caution and, occasionally, hostility when rendering first impressions.

Even now, when we're introduced to a visiting vice-president we'll immediately ask ourselves, "Do I like her? Do I trust her? And what's with those shoes?"

You know this. That's why you conducted your public relations outreach with scores of potential supporters *before* your presentation, and why you're going to work so hard on your connection with the audience early on.

You're going to smile. It's universally recognized to mean, "I'm friendly, not a threat, so relax already and let me sell you something."

A smile on the face of a well-turned-out corporate professional conveys a sense of confidence and goodwill. While a smile won't necessarily convince anyone that you have the goods, it does set the table for you to demonstrate them.

A scowl, on the other hand (which, for whatever irrational reason many speakers display right up until the moment they speak), denotes angst and antagonism. It makes observers feel uncomfortable. Thus, the glowering presenter operates at a disadvantage.

Authenticity always works; humour, only sometimes

Audiences want to be engaged by speakers whom they perceive as real, open, and affable. Leaders oblige. Whatever the circumstance, they get as close to their authentic selves as they can by interacting in a way that feels much like a conversation, personal, almost intimate. Some do it naturally, others by envisioning they're speaking to a group of close, trusted friends.

You can establish a bond with your listeners by sharing something of yourself, perhaps a recent experience that relates to the subject at hand. The earlier in your presentation you get personal, in a way that's not self-indulgent or self-aggrandizing but rather serves the needs of your listeners, the stronger your relationship with the audience is likely to become.

Concentrate on building rapport; but unless you're an experienced raconteur, avoid humour.

Why? There's an old saying that goes, "Three things can happen when you tell a joke, and two of them are bad."

Certainly, conventional, get-ready-for-the-punch-line humour can hit the mark, scoring significant points with your audience. But it can also bomb, being received so unfavourably as to approach the realm of career-limiting, or it can just fizzle, leaving listeners uneasy.

Why take the risk? If you must relate a joke, make it self-deprecating.

Above all else, in those first ninety seconds, be certain.

Audiences can quickly tell whether presenters are confident in their material or not. Self-doubt, ambiguity, and equivocation are killers; they'll flatten your credibility and influence. After all, if you're not sure, why should anyone else be?

A strong, definitive start communicates the fact that you're confident in your story, and, by extension, yourself.

Now, go get 'em.

IT'S ON!

It's 11:14 a.m. at "Industry 2020" in Las Vegas and you're on stage, being introduced.

It seems almost surreal.

All that planning. All that preparation. All those rehearsals — and here you are.

Your heart feels like it's going to burst out of your chest, it's pounding so hard. (Aren't you glad you didn't have that second cup of coffee?)

Your mouth feels like sandpaper, it's so dry. That's not just the desert air. It's nerves, and the fact that convention halls — wherever they're located — are notoriously dry. (Aren't you glad you've been sipping water? There's more, in a large glass, off to the side of the lectern. If you stay parched, by all means interrupt your presentation and take a sip. It's not a big deal.)

Nice introduction. Short and sweet, just like you prepared it for the conference.

Smile and the world smiles with you

Smile at the host as he introduces you, and make eye contact with a couple of friendly, supportive faces in the audience. There's your boss; she looks frazzled.

Smile at Peggy. Let her know it's going to be okay.

Keep smiling as the audience applauds.

You're at the lectern now, with your trusty three-ring binder. You're looking good, my friend.

Time to speak. With certainty.

Look at the host.

"Thank you, Tom."

Now look at the audience.

"Good morning."

Pause.

"It's great to be here with you in exciting Las Vegas."

Pretty good.

You purposely didn't say "Industry 2020." It's certainly not a complicated handle, but for whatever reason you slurred it, just so slightly, a couple of times in rehearsal and decided to jettison it for your introduction.

Smart move.

Keep your language simple and easy to pronounce, especially in the early going when you're naturally going to be more skittish.

Besides, presentation history is replete with speakers who've gotten the name of a conference or city or person wrong in the first few seconds, they were so nervous and distracted out of the box. Many had a difficult time recovering.

Be risk-averse.

The three previous speakers thanked the conference organizers and sponsors in their openings, but their expressions of appreciation went on too long and got tedious. The audience wanted them to cut to the chase, already.

So cut to the chase, already.

What can go wrong

"I want to thank our conference sponsor, [name the firm], for the opportunity to speak with you today. And I'd like to thank Peggy Pratt, our CEO and my mentor, for the privilege of sharing our corporate vision with you."

Now let your listeners know why what you're about to tell them will be important to them.

"Our industry has undergone a revolution. But it's just the beginning. Over the next decade, we'll experience even more changes, at every level of our business. Some of those changes will be profound. In fact, we can barely imagine them today. So how can we — my company and yours — possibly prepare for a future that's virtually impossible to envision? How can we stay relevant, let alone competitive, in an environment that's constantly shifting under our feet?"

You spent a lot of time preparing to deliver that paragraph, marking up your script — choreographing it — to give yourself the best chances of success.

You have your words printed only on the top half of each page, so there's no danger of your eyes drifting down to the bottom half and severing your connection with the audience.

Your script has been capitalized and bold-faced, with the words and phrases requiring special emphasis underlined.

There's no teleprompter available at "Industry 2020," at least not for you, so your script has taken on even more importance.

Here's what that first paragraph looks like in presentation format:

OUR INDUSTRY HAS UNDERGONE A <u>REVOLUTION</u>.

BUT IT'S JUST THE <u>BEGINNING</u>. (PAUSE)

OVER THE NEXT DECADE, WE'LL EXPERIENCE EVEN MORE CHANGES, AT <u>EVERY</u> LEVEL OF OUR BUSINESS.

SOME OF THOSE CHANGES WILL BE <u>PROFOUND</u>.

IN FACT, WE CAN BARELY <u>IMAGINE</u> THEM TODAY. (PAUSE)

SO HOW CAN <u>WE</u> — MY COMPANY AND <u>YOURS</u> — POSSIBLY PREPARE FOR A FUTURE THAT'S VIRTUALLY <u>IMPOSSIBLE</u> TO ENVISION?

HOW CAN WE STAY <u>RELEVANT</u> — LET ALONE <u>COMPETITIVE</u> — IN AN

ENVIRONMENT THAT'S CONSTANTLY
<u>SHIFTING</u> UNDER OUR FEET?

For all your preparation, you delivered those lines better in practice; they felt a bit rushed just now. What's more, the audience doesn't look as into you as you thought it would.

This is feeling different than it had in your mind.

Weird. Keep on.

"You know, when I started with my organization in 1993, email was considered cutting-edge technology and Bill Clinton was early in his first term as president. By the way, when I started with the company, I was six years old."

Ka-boom.

You had to go with the joke, didn't you?

Well, it didn't quite work out. You receive just a smattering of almost embarrassed laughter. "What's wrong with these people?" you think. "Are they dopey or something? They look half asleep! Why aren't they responding? Come on, this is good stuff!"

Who knows why some audiences are warm and receptive, while others are cold and skeptical? Even professional entertainers and performers don't have a clue; all they know is that when a group of people comes together, it forms a personality, and sometimes that personality can be a real piece of work.

This morning, for whatever reason, a difficult personality has congealed at "Industry 2020." You hadn't really noticed it with the three previous speakers. (Note to self: observe how other presenters are relating to the audience, or aren't. You might have been a little more prepared, psychologically, for this response.)

The bottom line is this: a minute and a half into your big presentation, you're in trouble.

It doesn't have to end this way. You have a choice here. You can ride your opening into the ground, taking your non-responsive listeners with you, or you can demonstrate the poise and acumen of an assured professional and employ techniques that turn the proceedings around.

The past doesn't define the future. Comprehensive preparation has provided you with options and given you the opportunity to save your presentation.

But first, you need to relax.

Manage your emotions

You may feel frantic, but your audience doesn't need to know that. Most nervousness doesn't show, so don't telegraph yours. Exhibit too many signs of anxiety and the crowd will begin to lose confidence in you and your message. Just about everyone gets a tad jittery delivering a presentation, especially if it gets off to a less-than-stellar start. That's natural.

But you need to control your nerves so they're not expressed through a high-pitched voice, shaking hands, and gratuitous apologies. Those expressions of angst invariably spell doom for a talk already in trouble. It's when you're under the most pressure that you need to appear the most composed.

If the first ninety seconds haven't gone particularly well, so be it. Put them behind you. You have many more seconds to be concerned about.

Re-group and name names

Take a long pause to get reoriented. (The silence might seem like an eternity to you, but don't worry.) Look down, contemplatively, not up, searchingly. Slow your breathing, your movement, and, when it comes time to speak, your delivery.

Your most pressing task is to re-engage your listeners. How? Make it about them. If you had any conversations with conference attendees the previous day that are relevant to the material you're about to deliver, refer to them as you move forward (aren't you glad you arrived in Vegas early?).

"I was speaking with David Holmes of Dallas yesterday about the challenges we face in this industry, and we agreed that while sometimes they appear daunting, we also agreed that they're loaded with opportunity."

What do you think David Holmes of Dallas will do when he hears his name? Why, his ears will prick up, and he'll lean forward. He'll nod and smile. He'll throw his attention and support behind you. So will those who know and like David.

But don't stop there.

"Connie Henderson of New York also had some fascinating insights on this subject. Connie, we're very much looking forward to your workshop this afternoon."

Connie will be ready to give you a standing ovation. Now.

Use two names, three at most, or the outreach will come off as manipulative and self-serving. Your goal is to involve your listeners so they feel part of your presentation, so they feel as if they have a stake in your success.

Relieve the pressure on yourself

Often, when we're failing in a presentation — or believe we are — it's because we've made the interaction too much about ourselves. It seems like a one-sided performance, but listeners want to feel as if they're part of a dialogue in which their views matter.

That can take a great deal of pressure off the speaker.

So, relieve the pressure.

Ask a question.

It doesn't have to be profound, but it does have to be posed sincerely, and you actually have to be interested in the answer. With a well-asked question, you can begin to replicate the early trajectory of an authentic conversation and start involving the audience.

In presentations, shortly after I've been introduced, I'll often ask if anyone in the audience attended Acadia

University, my alma mater. Usually, someone will put up a hand.

I'll find out what year the person graduated, and then make a joke about the two of us representing different generations of Acadia alumni. Okay, I'm not Chris Rock, but the remark usually gets a laugh.

More importantly, it warms the room and establishes a connection.

Questions can be great, but don't overdo them.

Asking three or four questions over the course of a keynote presentation is fine, but three or four questions in a row rarely works, unless they're leading impressively and strategically to a sharp conclusion, and you ask them extraordinarily well.

For non-professionals, it's best to proceed more deliberately, working the audience's answer into your ongoing narrative.

Now, if it so happens that you can't see individual members of the audience, which can happen in large, darkened conference halls, you obviously won't be able to see any raised hands in response to your question. The solution: you'll have to ask a question of yourself, playing the role of both interviewer and expert.

This is where you have to step up your game. You can't be tentative here. For the audience to buy into the validity of your question and response, you have to sell it with an energetic, at times theatrical, turn.

Like every other element of delivering an effective presentation, extricating yourself from a challenging spot requires preparation.

Just before you left for Las Vegas you came across a hilarious digital clip, less than twenty seconds in length, that you thought would go down very well here. Peggy agreed, but neither of you were sure exactly where it would fit in your presentation. Nevertheless, with Peggy's permission you had it embedded in your Power-Point (along with the seventy-five-second clip of your customer interviews), just in case you needed it.

You need it. You're in a jam.

Play it to energize the audience, lighten the atmosphere, and give yourself a break.

There's more you can do to recover from a middling start.

Display a prop or reveal a mystery product or campaign. Human beings are insatiably curious. You'll have them at, "What do you think this is?"

That old standby, the common flip chart, makes for a great dramatic vehicle. You could always have one positioned on the stage, fairly close by, with the answer to the question you're about to ask your listeners written in bold letters large enough for the entire audience to see. Perhaps the word, inscribed on the second sheet of the flip chart (you want the top sheet to be blank), reads: MONEY

You could then ask the audience, "What does it really come down to?"

You could solicit a few responses, and, without saying a word, walk over to the flip chart, where, with a flourish, you'd throw over the top sheet and reveal the word: MONEY.

"Theresa is exactly right. It's all about the money."

Be creative. You're the speaker. You're in charge. And the pleasant irony is, the more power you give to your listeners, the more will come back to you.

Thorough preparation prevents most presentations from going bad. But despite how well you prepare, challenges will occur. Maybe you'll be slightly off — it happens to the best speakers in the world. Perhaps your audience will be strangely unresponsive or distracted; sometimes that collective mindset has nothing to do with you.

Whatever the dynamics, hang in there like grit. Keep trying to connect with your listeners — they'll respect you for it. And however rough the ride becomes, be thankful for it.

It's making you a better presenter.

Ten Questions You Can Ask an Audience

1. How many of you have children?
2. When it comes to your business, what's your biggest fear?
3. What's your top business priority today?
4. What's the most pressing need of people in the workplace today?
5. What's the main quality you're looking for in a business partner?
6. What's the one thing you do better than your competitors?

7. What's one thing you wish you had done better in your business over the last year?

8. Why do you think this initiative succeeded?

9. Looking ahead ten years, where will your business be?

10. When you look back over your career, what's the one thing you're most proud of?

The Third Key — Passion

You've recovered beautifully from your challenging start. You're hitting your stride.

The fun clip altered the atmosphere in the conference hall and contributed to a more positive vibe. It also bought you some time to re-group and think about ways in which you can make your presentation more of a shared experience, in which the audience has a stake.

YOU'RE ALL IN THIS TOGETHER

There's another reason why you're connecting more effectively: you're speaking with passion. You're feeling it, and so are your listeners. They can tell you care deeply about your subject, and that you believe in the vision your company has embraced.

You can't speak like a leader without passion. No one can.

In presentation skills sessions, when participants are asked what makes for a great speech they invariably respond: passion.

They're right, of course. You can have the best presentation ever crafted, but if you don't have passion, you have nothing.

A legend of the lectern

When I think of passion, I think of a speech given on May 14, 1980, in Montreal by Canadian Prime Minister Pierre Trudeau, leading the fight against Quebec independence.

His passion was palpable.

His eyes burning with emotion, Trudeau roared, "These people in Quebec and in Canada want to split it up? They want to take it away from their children? They want to break it down? No! That's our answer."

Orator Obama — Michelle Obama

When I think of passion, I think of Michelle Obama, introducing her husband, then a candidate for the Democratic Party's presidential nomination, at a campaign event in Des Moines, Iowa in August 2007.

Mrs. Obama spoke on the theme that after years of Republican fear-mongering, she and millions of other Americans were "tired of being afraid."

She was open, personal, and her listeners at the Iowa State Fair were rapt. Mrs. Obama spoke to them as a wife, mother, and citizen, reaching them on every level — intellectual, emotional, and political.

Her delivery wasn't flawless. In fact, her narrative was marked by several "ahs." But I guarantee you, no one cared; she was so obviously locked in, so giving of herself, achieving that sublime connection that occurs so rarely in public presentations.

"Whenever I get in front of an audience I get pumped up," she said, "because I'm very passionate about this race. I'm passionate about my husband in this race. Because I know that, and I'm trying to convey to all of you, that there is something very special about this man."

Michelle Obama's remarks that day can serve as an example for anyone wanting to become an inspiring speaker, but it was especially instructive for women, many of whom believe that when it comes to addressing others, they're subject to more scrutiny, skepticism, and criticism than men.

Women have always had to walk a narrower line in their careers. But a lot of female presenters frequently work against themselves too, repeating mistakes that virtually invite their audiences to discount them.

Accomplished orators like Mrs. Obama rarely undermine themselves. They do the same things well, and consistently. Here's how women — anyone, really — can speak with poise and self-assurance, just like the First Lady of the United States.

Expect success

Women are generally more aware of the emotional atmosphere — the mood — of a room than men. If it's negative, women speakers tend to pick up on it more quickly and deal with it less confidently.

I have a friend, a forty-something woman in Philadelphia, with a high-profile job in the pharmaceutical industry. She believes that women have to guard against internalizing the negativity they perceive in the odd listener.

"Forget the energy-drainer," she says. "Find the smile."

It's excellent advice for women and men. Besides, the audience member glowering at you may be doing so for reasons totally unrelated to you, you just happen to be in the way. He may be sick or have daunting personal issues. You can't make his unhappiness your insecurity.

Speakers who demand respect from their audiences, however unenthusiastic and restless at the outset, invariably get it. Those who don't, won't.

Steel yourself for success before every presentation. Don't let it be dependent on the disposition of your listeners. Serve their informational needs with self-assurance, and you'll usually transform their frame of mind.

Inflect down

In intimate conversation with family and friends, women will often inflect their voices up at the end of sentences to engage others in a considerate way. But strengths in private can be weaknesses in public.

The tendency to "talk up" — often described derisively as "up talk" — works against women professionally. It makes them appear less convincing and credible (and occasionally sound like the seventeen-year-old clerk who works at my local video store).

When you inflect down, on the other hand, you communicate confidence and conviction.

All presenters need to inflect down at the end of their sentences, except when they're asking a question of the audience or themselves. If you need a reminder, mark your script with an arrow pointing down at the end of every statement.

Speak up

Don't let your voice go faint or falter.

In a smaller room, without audio support, project loudly enough so that the listeners who are farthest away can hear you. Do a quick sound check with colleagues or early arrivals before commencing your formal remarks.

At conferences, go with a lavaliere microphone, which will free you to move and look like a leader. If you have an option, don't stay rooted to the lectern or your laptop.

Don't apologize unnecessarily

There's an adage in presentation skills coaching that dictates that a speaker should never apologize. I'd revise the maxim to read "most of the time."

If you mess up badly, it would be ungracious not to ask for forgiveness. However, resist the urge to apologize unnecessarily and gratuitously, it's irritating and distracting to an audience.

If you flub a line, correct yourself and move on without comment.

If your technology goes down, fix it — or ditch it — and keep going.

If you lose your place, consult your notes in silence and pick up your narrative again.

No one is infallible. Your listeners get this. You should too.

Choose professionalism over fashion

The percentages vary, but experts agree that the visual component of interpersonal communication comprises at least 70 percent of an audience's total perception. In other words, how you look and move is more important than what you say.

There's no doubt about it. Appearance is important, and that can be a special challenge for women. Why? Because there are more elements to a woman's appearance — from hair and makeup to jewellery and clothing — that have the potential to distract, and thus detract.

If listeners are gazing at your dangling earrings or sheer, colourful designer blouse, chances are they're not fully absorbing what you have to say, or, worse, they're marginalizing what you have to say.

The best female speakers eliminate potential distractions. They wear little makeup and jewellery, and select stylish, well-tailored ensembles appropriate for the occasion.

"There's a fine line between fashion and professionalism," says a prominent female public relations executive in Toronto. "Women should never let fashion take away from their professionalism."

Don't nod unless you mean to

Responsive listeners tend to nod out of approval or support when carefully tracking other people's narratives. That's fine, unless you're in a question-and-answer session and nodding affirmatively to a query that may have a circuitous trajectory and a negative-based outcome.

Be attentive and open, but relatively stationary when a question is being asked. You never know where it might be heading.

Observe the best

Presentation skills, as with any other discipline, get better with practice and observation.

Watch Michelle Obama and you'll learn a lot about effective communication. She may well be a better speaker than her husband.

KEEP THE FOCUS ON YOUR LISTENERS

You're seven minutes into your presentation, and you're doing well.

You've smoothly made the transition from your introduction to the first of your three body points on your company's products, and the audience appears to be solidly with you.

"Hey," you say to yourself. "I'm doing great!"

Wrong sentiment.

Whenever I've complimented myself during a presentation (silently, of course), it means I've lost focus. It means I've made the interaction too much about me.

The question every presenter should be asking isn't, "How am I doing?"

It should be, "How are *they* doing? How are my listeners doing?"

All great speakers ask that question of themselves several times during a presentation. Operating at an extraordinary high level of human interaction, they can tighten and shorten sections that aren't fully resonating with the crowd, and bulk up parts that are, with more facts, examples, and anecdotes.

Audiences will tell you what they want, you just have to be paying attention.

A superb communicator

Being attuned to the informational and emotional needs of your audience and speaking to them passionately is the mark of an exceptional communicator.

It describes Ron Ellis, a former star forward with the Toronto Maple Leafs.

Ellis played for the Leafs over sixteen National Hockey

League seasons, before his second and final retirement from the game in the early 1980s. He attributes his first retirement, in the mid-1970s, to the depression he's battled most of his adult life. He was hospitalized three times with the illness.

Mr. Ellis has successfully managed his depression for many years, through medication, therapy, strong family support, and his faith. But rather than keep his experiences with the disease private, he's chosen to reveal them. In doing so, he contributes awareness, education, and hope.

At a reception in January 2001, Mr. Ellis gave the best speech I've ever heard. It was stunning in its construction, delivery, and impact.

In simple language, without a hint of embellishment, self-interest, or self-pity, he told the story of his life and how it has been affected by depression. Ellis encouraged his listeners to acknowledge their own attitudes about mental illness, and called upon organizations to treat employees who suffer from the disease with the same sensitivity, respect, and encouragement that his long-time employer, the Hockey Hall of Fame, has shown him.

His remarks literally rocked the room.

The expression of passion, with the interests of your audience at its core, can be magnetic. The expression of passion, without knowing or caring anything about your audience, cannot. It qualifies, in fact, as self-aggrandizement. We saw a lot of that in business in the years leading up to and including 2008, when the world's financial system came perilously close to melting down.

Today, thankfully, more executives are returning to the old communication values, which dictate that when you serve the needs of your listeners with concern and passion, you'll be rewarded beyond all measure.

To get there, you need to be continually checking in. You need to be asking, "How are *they* doing?"

THE HAZARDS OF HUMOUR

Like most people, I'm a fan of self-deprecating humour in presentations. My advice is to be very careful with any humour that isn't.

That's because I've seen and heard so many examples of material that speakers considered funny coming back to hurt them and their organizations.

The inappropriate joke you tell at a small conference in upstate New York can be recorded and uploaded to the Internet, where it can go viral and take on perpetual life, undermining your reputation on an hourly basis.

Here's how to protect yourself, and use humor judiciously.

First, decide if you really need it

If you're an inexperienced speaker, or someone who lacks confidence when addressing others, forget about using humour until you're far more secure at the lectern or in the meeting room.

You don't need humour to give a successful presentation.

Besides, preparing to deliver a joke with just the right degree of timing and emphasis takes up a lot of mental capacity. It can distract you from delivering, with assurance, the narrative that comes before (what you hope will be) an amusing quip.

Humour is a high-risk operation for the inexperienced. They almost never recover from a joke that goes over badly in the early going — and neither does their audience.

Know your audience

You really have to know a great deal about your listeners before attempting humour.

Do they have all the background or contextual information required to understand the joke you plan to tell? What's their state of mind? Are they relaxed at a retreat, or tense at a sales meeting?

Is there the potential for even a few listeners to be offended?

If you can't answer those questions, or if you have any doubts, opt for caution and ditch your routine.

Know the rules

We live in a multicultural, politically sensitive society that's increasingly intolerant of crude, abusive humour.

You don't joke about an incident if people have died or become ill. You don't joke about those with physical or intellectual disabilities. You don't joke about religion and you don't joke about anyone's appearance.

If you're thinking about dispensing humour at a professional venue, large or small, test it beforehand on several trusted colleagues, preferably of both genders and of different ethnic backgrounds. You may be surprised by how they react.

If you offend, apologize immediately

I conduct more than eighty communication skills sessions a year, so I know better than most that if you talk long enough to enough people, you're bound to say something stupid.

The best thing you can do when that happens is to apologize, as soon as you can.

Appearing on *The Tonight Show* with Jay Leno in March 2009, President Obama made a terrible joke at the expense of those with intellectual disabilities. Speaking about his recent low bowling score of 129, he said, "It was like Special Olympics or something."

Mr. Obama appeared distracted for the remainder of the interview; he knew he'd erred badly. After the taping of the show, on his way back to Washington on Air Force One, the President called the chairman of the Special Olympics, Timothy Shriver, to apologize.

"He was sincere and heartfelt," said Mr. Shriver, in a statement the next day. It was, he said, "a teachable moment."

LOW-RISK HUMOUR

In April 2006 Prime Minister Stephen Harper did something that Canadian politicians rarely do, at least publicly.

He made a self-deprecating joke. And it worked.

In the House of Commons, NDP MP Pat Martin accused Mr. Harper of having "seduced" former Liberal David Emerson into the Conservative Cabinet. Mr. Harper replied, "Mr. Speaker, I don't think I've been accused of ever seducing anyone, even my wife."

With his wife, Laureen, watching from the visitors' gallery, he added, "I see there's some agreement in the gallery."

Nightclub timing

Mr. Harper's remarks, delivered with the exquisite timing of a veteran Las Vegas nightclub performer, produced some big laughs in the House — and outside it. The media picked up and disseminated the prime minister's standup routine to millions across the country. They received a warmer, more appealing view of the oft-solemn man who leads them.

Such is the power of self-deprecating humour: in a few words it can lighten and uplift, alleviate and loosen.

Those who can laugh at themselves, we figure, are emotionally balanced, confident, and likeable — reassuringly human. When the self-deprecation comes from a leader, it packs even more of a punch.

Delivered in a presentation, it can be funny and charming. Expressed in the workplace, it can be downright stirring, demonstrating to employees that their chief executive officers, managers, and supervisors are genuine, down-to-earth folks, just like them.

Good-natured self-deprecation isn't used nearly enough in our grimly proper political and business worlds, where self-justification and self-importance are far more likely to be expressed. It's a terrific option for speakers, much less risky than punchline humour, which, as we've learned, can become a story all its own.

As with all communication, though, there are guidelines to follow if you want to make self-deprecating humour work successfully.

It has to be real

A self-deprecating reference is only amusing if it springs off some truth or perception. For example, because many believe Mr. Harper to be cold, remote, and even repressed, he was able to lampoon the notion that he could seduce anyone.

In the self-deprecation game, you must riff off of reality.

Know your audience — and yourself

You may consider your planned remark hilarious, but will your listeners get it? They'll need to know enough about you to discern the self-deprecating humour. The better you know your audience, the better you'll understand how much context to provide before delivering your lines.

If you're at all uncertain, don't force the self-deprecating patter. Focus instead on serving your listeners. Over time, the great material will come, sometimes spontaneously.

Deliver the goods

Self-deprecating humour can be potent stuff. You want to make sure that everyone gets in on the joke.

That means infusing your lines with a pause, a smile, and strong intonation, the slower the better. Delivery is important, but content is king.

Consider the self-deprecating content employed by legendary former General Electric CEO Jack Welch, ruminating on GE's painful foray into a business about which it had no clue — investment banking — with its 1986 purchase of brokerage firm Kidder, Peabody & Co. Inc.

The deal was conceived amid remarkable hubris, when GE was on an acquisition high.

"I was on a roll," said the short, bald Mr. Welch. "I thought I was six foot four with hair."

LOVE THE POINT YOU'RE WITH

You're twelve minutes into your keynote presentation at "Industry 2020," almost halfway through, and you've hit a flat spot.

It happens.

You're early in your explanation of body point two, on your company's partnerships, which you're less keen on than you were the first point (and will be on the third) and it's showing.

You know, though, that you need to make every point count. You also know that your CEO has a special interest in point two; in fact, she specifically requested that it be included. (And you like your job.)

How do you communicate passion when you don't feel particularly passionate about a section of a presentation, or even an entire presentation?

It's simple: you have to find the love.

You have to find some element of the material that you adore or fervently believe in or can bring to life with a personal experience or insight.

No one says you have to spend as much time on point two as you do the others, but you do have to make it "stick." The audience expects and deserves your full effort on every point.

To make a point stick, keep your sentences short and declarative. Leave plenty of space, in the form of pauses, between them and identify at least one key word or phrase in every sentence that you can accentuate, or, as they say in the presentation skills business, "punch out."

That will infuse your delivery with the inflection required of all effective presenters. It's a technique that's especially helpful for those more likely to speak in a monotone.

What else can you do to generate and communicate passion?

You can move.

The magic of movement

The best speakers around are frequently on the go.

Dependable wireless microphone technology enables them to roam. They pace their respective stages, pausing, reflecting, gesturing, their voices rising and falling with the import of their words, their words consistent with their movement.

Real people move. So why wouldn't you move when you speak?

Today, headliners on the big time U.S. speaking circuit will, more often than not, take flight. When they do hit the road, it can be magic. Few things compel audiences like passionate, well-prepared presenters who move in tandem with their narrative.

It wasn't so long ago that business and political leaders delivered speeches as if hammered into place at their lecterns, all stiff and unbending.

The resulting scenes — overly formal speakers rendered immobile by logistics and convention — seem immeasurably dated today. There's a premium now on naturalness and openness, on revealing something of yourself as you engage the audience.

Take flight only when it's right

Movement works well for many speakers, but not all.

Politicians, for example, still have far less opportunity for mobility, for reasons of security and television's requirement for stable, clean head-and-shoulder shots. Yet increasingly, political figures like President Obama are taking advantage of town hall meetings to more intimately connect with their audiences.

A lot depends on your vocation and the venue.

While a speaker's walk usually goes down well at industry conferences, sales meetings, and motivational seminars, it wouldn't be acceptable for a State of the Union address, an announcement of employee layoffs, or a news briefing on, say, a power outage.

When the occasion is right, however, it's great to travel. Your "journey" may be limited to a few steps, or it could be as far-reaching as an expedition deep into the recesses of a packed auditorium. It depends on logistics, technology, and your degree of comfort.

Confident speakers move. They pause. They smile, forever keeping in mind that their presentation represents simple human interaction. Presenters who lack confidence repress themselves, and their inclination to stir even a modicum. They reason, "If I move, I'll have to reveal even more of myself."

Exactly.

If you want to fully express your passion as a speaker, you have to move when the circumstances are right. Here's how.

Establish your presence

Don't hit the road right away. Be relatively stationary, but not still, for the first ninety seconds — remember how important they are. Establish your purpose with the audience from your "beach head" at the lectern (or, in a meeting, at the head of the conference table) with your laptop and notes.

Your listeners need to get oriented to you and your message in the early going, so don't overwhelm them with rapid-fire patter and motion. Be calm and unhurried, outlining what's to come. Then you can take off.

Learn to balance

Just the act of stepping a few metres away from the lectern to share an anecdote or expand upon a point communicates poise, panache, and personality. You're saying, in effect, "I have the confidence to move, to be real."

As you approach the individuals on your route, make eye contact, but don't forget the larger audience; it requires your attention, too. This necessitates a fine balance — telling your story in an absorbing manner as you walk, maintaining a relationship with those in your path and beyond, all the while restricting the amount of time each section of listeners views your back.

Expand your zone

How do you move when the world so often seems intent on keeping you stationary? How do you possibly integrate action when there's no stage to traverse, and no lavaliere microphone to free you? You can expand your delivery zone.

If you're confined to a lectern with a microphone, you can lean slightly forward or move to either side when accentuating key points (but only after conducting a pre-presentation sound check to ensure your voice will be picked up).

And remember the old reliable flip chart. For dramatic effect you can always stride over to the trusty apparatus and reveal a number or an answer or a slogan that drives home a point. But when you walk, walk silently. Bring some mystery to your movement.

Be prepared for the challenges

Eight years ago I was speaking to a group of pharmaceutical executives in Florida when something in the room distracted me, and my mind went vacant. It will do that on occasion. There I was, having wandered into a sea of forty high-flyers, quite lost, with no notes, of course.

(Never carry paper while you're speaking. You'll look like the manager of a discount department store.)

Guess what? My listeners didn't notice. I paused, which looked thoughtful, and then asked a question. Several voices piped up with answers that fit neatly into the points I'd been making and all was well.

Life can certainly be more stressful in the field, but the rewards of presenting on the go far outweigh the risks. Besides, if you get stuck, you can always ask a question.

Now, when are you going to start moving?

SAY NO TO NEGATIVITY

Speaking to five hundred people is much like being in a relationship.

It takes a lot of effort to make it work, and sometimes you just get tired.

That's the way you're feeling now, eighteen minutes into your speech, fairly deep in the explanation of point three, which is about your company's people. You're feeling the effects of the pressure, the preparation, the travel, the expectations, and the scrutiny.

You're feeling fatigued.

It's understandable.

Speaking with passion to a group of listeners, large or small, requires a ton of energy, which, on occasion, is bound to flag.

So what can you do to revive yourself for the home stretch?

Take a pause. Have a sip of water. Ask a question. Employ ultra-short sentences. Slow your delivery. Emphasize key words and phrases.

What you should never do is give any indication to your audience that you're wearying. Some speakers, incomprehensively, will say, "I'm tired," or "I'm really feeling this head cold," or "I didn't get into my hotel room until three o'clock this morning."

News flash: no one cares.

It's harsh but true. If you're feeling well enough to pull yourself up to the lectern, you're well enough to speak without complaint.

Remember that any negative-based comments, true or not, are guaranteed to stick in the minds of listeners long after your presentation, and continue to undermine their perception of your remarks.

What you need here is some "jump" in your narrative. A strong, quotable statement can provide it.

Go for the quote

It seems that few speakers give a great quote anymore.

We're buried under a growing mound of news, opinion, and perspective, but the expanding quantity of information hasn't been matched by a corresponding increase in creativity or even originality.

In fact, the opposite has occurred — with a few notable exceptions, the calibre of public expression has diminished. In writing and in speech, it's taken on a desultory sameness, a predictable repetition of the obvious and the inoffensive.

The great quote, a passage that encapsulates an opinion or belief, has been a casualty of the decline.

Winston Churchill once called fellow British politician Clement Atlee "a sheep in sheep's clothing." These decades later, the crack still rings with derision.

Churchill employed words to ridicule, but more importantly he used them to inspire and to lead. Consider his defiance as prime minister following the British retreat from Dunkirk, France in June 1940. "We shall fight on the beaches," he told his House of Commons, "we shall fight on the landing grounds, we shall fight in the fields and in the streets, we shall fight in the hills; we shall never surrender."

Churchill understood that a great quote wields remarkable power, far beyond the sum of the words deployed. In a world flush with confluences and contradictions, it stands for something. It represents a point of view.

A quote cuts through

A strong, clear, provocative quote means you have something to say, which is why such passages appear to be in limited supply these days. Political correctness has caused us to constrict the range and power of our wonderful English language and incapacitate our own opinions.

As we trip all over ourselves in an attempt not to offend anyone (or any thing for that matter), we find refuge in the banal, sanitized "public speak" of the intelligentsia

— thus, the tiring overuse of approved words like consultation, inclusion, and, disturbingly, organic.

At social events, when an aloof, balding, black-clad advertising type uses the word *organic* to describe the nature of his groundbreaking campaign for an exciting new line of, say, soap products, I always ask what he means when he says *organic*. I wait as long as it takes for a coherent response. (There's usually enough time to drink several beverages — and occasionally fill out a mortgage application.)

Then there are the pretentious and ultimately inane corporate expressions such as core competencies, value-added, win-win, results-driven, and strategic alignment.

Not quite quote-worthy.

To influence others you need to believe in your story. To bring your story fully to life you need a first-rate quote.

Quotes stand out — and up

"There's no place for the state in the bedrooms of the nation," said then Justice Minister Pierre Trudeau in 1967. This statement expressed his government's position on decriminalizing "homosexual acts" in a way that all Canadians could understand.

Combining simplicity and persuasion, great quotes do the job when required and hold up superbly over time.

"As I would not be a slave," said future U.S. President Abraham Lincoln in 1858, "so I would not be a master. This expresses my idea of democracy."

That the memorable quote has largely disappeared from contemporary business and political life represents both a failure of collective confidence and an opportunity for differentiation.

You can stand out from the crowd with a great quote. A robust, evocative passage serves those who deal with the media especially well. A hot quote is catnip to reporters; they have a hard time resisting it. They're almost forced to use it.

How can you create a winning quote that reflects your theme while providing your presentation with jump — that injection of passion — when you require it?

Open your imagination

Think outside the margins, like you did as a kid.

To get started use similes, which compare one thing with another of a different kind (for example: "He's as meek as a mouse").

There are no bad ideas in this exercise. You may create scores of versions before you hit on one that sizzles. A great quote takes a lot of work.

Test it

Often, an analogy makes for a memorable quote.

"I am a Ford," said Gerald Ford, upon taking the oath of U.S. vice-president in 1973, "not a Lincoln."

Whatever your passage, test it on colleagues before the release date. Make sure it has the effect you intended. Sometimes, you'll get a perspective you hadn't considered.

Be wary of the negative quote

The Ford quote is interesting, because in comparing himself to Lincoln, the greatest president, Ford nevertheless placed limitations on himself and others' expectations of him.

Did that help him during his presidency?

Probably not.

Be careful. A quote can be read multiple ways. Make sure yours can't be misconstrued or decontextualized.

"I'm not a crook," said President Richard Nixon in November 1973, the words for which he's most remembered.

In an hour-long question-and-answer session with 400 Associated Press managing editors in Orlando, Florida, Nixon said, "People have got to know whether or not their President is a crook. Well, I'm not a crook. I've earned everything I've got."

"I did not have sexual relations with that woman, Miss Lewinsky," said President Bill Clinton, the words for which he'll likely be most remembered.

In January 1998, at the conclusion of his prepared remarks on education policy proposals, Clinton said, "Now, I have to go back to work on my State of the Union speech. And I worked on it until pretty late last night. But I want to say one thing to the American people. I want you to listen to me. I'm going to say this again. I did not have sexual relations with that woman, Miss Lewinsky. I never told anybody to lie, not a single time — never. These allegations are false. And I need to go back to work for the American people. Thank you."

Incredible, isn't it? Negatives, within quotes and outside them, can exert a power that extends through the generations.

Excel in your delivery

When giving a presentation that includes a significant quote, let the crowd know that something special is on the way: pause beforehand, then, slowly drive the passage home, accentuating every word of it.

If you fail to flag your quote and end up delivering it with the same emphasis as you do other parts of your narrative, the audience may be uncertain about its importance.

You've worked hard on your quote. Make it count.

THE STRETCH RUN

Life is good, twenty-one minutes into your big presentation at "Industry 2020," as you prepare to roll into your conclusion.

Your quote did the job.

It wasn't the most original passage in the world, but you delivered it well — with passion — and the audience was all over it.

"Our company believes in the future," you said, "we just wish it would hurry up and get here."

Nicely done, my friend. Way to hang in there when you perceived the going got flat. Now you're reaping the rewards.

Peggy, the CEO who's rapidly becoming a big fan of yours, loved it. You could see her beaming, just like a proud parent, from row eight.

The value of vision

Being able to speak about your company vision has been a decided advantage for you at "Industry 2020." The future, in the parlance of communication types, is a sexy subject. Audiences get excited about it.

It has to do with "the vision thing."

That's what U.S. Vice-President George H.W. Bush called it, somewhat dismissively, during the 1988 Presidential election campaign.

Bush won in '88, but lost in '92.

Leaders need to talk vision, which, when passionately created and steadfastly applied, can remake a city, a country, and certainly a company.

So why is there such a lack of vision these days?

Why do so many of those in positions of leadership fail to provide a clear, exhilarating image of where they want to take us, and why they want to take us there?

Leaders communicate vision

Most leaders who fail do so because they either have no clue, or, if they do know, decline to disclose the information for fear that few would fall in behind them. Yet there's no way around it — to be a standout leader you need to express vision.

"I believe," President John F. Kennedy told a Joint Session of Congress in 1961, "this nation should commit itself to achieving the goal, before this decade is out, of landing a man on the moon and returning him safely to the Earth."

Kennedy's statement was met with incredulity by large numbers of the American public. Nevertheless, on July 20, 1969, Neil Armstrong walked on the surface of the moon.

JFK wasn't around to see it, of course, having been assassinated in Dallas on November 22, 1963. But his transcendent call to action survived him and became astonishing science fiction reality.

Kennedy had vision. The best leaders always do.

As a motivational junkie, I find the importance of vision a theme that's consistently emphasized in the tapes, DVDs, and videos I listen to.

My favourite phrase, with which I regale (and quite possibly bore) friends and clients, theorizes that vision lies at the core of most success: You become what you think about.

It's been said that we can achieve virtually anything we choose, if we could only decide what that is. With a surfeit of opportunities and challenges, insecurities and distractions, many people struggle to determine exactly who it is they wish to become — in their careers and outside them — and what the outcome looks like in their mind.

If they settled all that, they'd be more than halfway there.

Purpose brings clarity and clarity produces vision, a well-delineated blueprint for your life. When opportunities do come along, you're then able to evaluate them according to your plan and confidently make the right decision.

If the opportunity fits with your vision, you take it. If it doesn't, you don't.

Once you've set in place a full, luminous vision, the world itself will seem to cooperate. Each day, you'll move closer to your objective, often without even realizing it. That's the stunning power of vision, as essential for business entities as for individuals.

How do you create your vision?

It starts with rigorous self-analysis, which can be disconcerting and painful. It's also widely resisted in our syrupy "everything we do is fantastic" world. We need to find what we were put on the planet to do, and then do it.

There's nothing sadder than speaking with elderly men and women who spent their lives in jobs they loathed. While many of them had few options, those who did lament the fact they didn't take more risks and go after their dreams.

Vision is many things — most of all, it's courage.

STRONG CLOSE, STRONG WORDS

As you head into the conclusion, your listeners need to hear your passion.

They need to feel it, too.

So many presentations fall apart at the end. It's as if speakers run out of gas or interest or both.

During the planning process, there's a tendency for presenters to blow off the conclusion, assuming that it will somehow take care of itself.

It doesn't.

How many times have you seen a speaker falter in the final stretch, stumped (and sometimes unnerved) about how to wrap up? Hours of preparation can go down the tubes with a wonky conclusion, along with much of the credibility a speaker has stockpiled throughout the presentation.

That's not going to happen to you here at "Industry 2020."

You've learned your narrative from the outside in, committing the introduction and conclusion virtually to memory, and providing yourself with a huge dose of security.

Consider how much weaker your introduction would have been without that level of preparation. Okay, so you didn't shoot the lights out with your opening remarks. The conclusion will be different — you can feel it. You've learned a lot in the last twenty-one minutes, and that education is about to pay off.

Deal in definitive language

In the telling of your story, you've employed convincing, authoritative language, such as "we will," "we have," and "we're committed."

You've avoided weak, tentative vocabulary, such as "try," "maybe," and that wimpiest, most namby-pamby word of all, "hope."

You haven't equivocated in twenty-one minutes. You're not going to start now.

By speaking definitively, you can stand apart from the crowd.

Over the last generation, since schmooze-loving

baby boomers began assuming positions of authority in business, government, and education, there's been a movement to soften any language that runs the risk of being too frank and potentially offensive to someone. Anyone. Anywhere.

A perfect example of this dismal, misguided form of communication occurred in January 2009, when Ontario Premier Dalton McGuinty commented on a long-running strike by teaching assistants at York University.

"Let's not kid ourselves," said McGuinty, "York has sustained a bit of a black eye."

Well, you either have a black eye, or you don't.

Other weak-kneed expressions include "kind of," "sort of," and "I guess."

Forgive the cliché, but don't pull your punches. If you have something to say, attempting to weaken it with the phrase "a bit of" doesn't help your case, or your standing. All it means is that you're not speaking like a leader.

The conclusion especially is where your language needs to be unequivocal, loaded with positive "power" words that evoke strong emotion and resonate in the minds of your listeners. The end is no place for weak, negative-based communication, unless, for some reason, it's the last — and lasting — impression you want to leave with your audience.

Take great care in the selection of your vocabulary. Positive and negative words can influence the outcome of your conclusion in entirely different ways. Indeed, they can influence the perception of an entire presentation.

Here are some potent positive and negative words for your consideration:

POSITIVE WORDS	NEGATIVE WORDS
Ability	Alleged
Accomplish	Bailout
Achieve	Biased
Approve	Blame
Believe	Can't
Benefit	Collusion
Can	Confuse
Children	Contradict
Clean	Decline
Commit	Defeat
Country	Deficit
Enhance	Disappoint
Family	Dispute
Great	Error
Improve	Excuse
Lead	Fail
Love	Insurmountable
Mother	Miss
Optimism	Obstacle
Protect	Peril
Reliable	Problem
Safe	Tired
Success	Wasteful
Value	Weak
You	Wrong

As you begin your conclusion, put any flubs, mistakes, or concerns behind you.

Determine to make the next four minutes special, and whatever you do, revel in the experience.

Be in the moment. It's how leaders speak.

The Fourth Key — Engagement

You rocked the room with your close.

You tied your story together, briefly reviewed the key points of your presentation, and invited the audience to join you and your company in embracing your industry's future.

"I've spoken about my organization's vision for our products, partnerships, and people," you said.

> I can tell you that my colleagues and I are greatly excited about the prospects for our company, and for our sector.
>
> You know, all of us in his room are very fortunate to do what we do for a living. We work in

a vibrant, challenging business. It's a great place to build a career.

All of us have a stake in continuing to attract smart, motivated young people to the industry. It's an important priority, and one to which my company is committed.

For this reason, I'm delighted to announce that my organization has established an "Industry 2020" scholarship, to honour this conference — to mark our coming together — here in Las Vegas.

The scholarship will be awarded annually to a promising university or college student from across the country. That student will receive a generous stipend, as well as full benefits, for a year to further his or her education at a postgraduate institution of their choice. And when the student completes the year of study, there will be a job in our industry waiting — perhaps even with your company.

This outstanding scholarship is the brainchild of our company CEO, Peggy Pratt. Peggy, thank you.

Here, you left plenty of time for the audience to acknowledge Peggy with applause.

I invite you to nominate an exceptional student in your area for consideration by the scholarship committee.

Ladies and gentlemen, when it comes right down to it, we're all in this together, contributing to an industry that's among the finest in the world.

We can learn from each other. We can help each other. There's plenty of business out there for everyone. And it's only going to grow.

Let's embrace the future together.

The year 2020 is on the way.

Thank you.

Nicely done!

As your listeners acknowledge you with an animated ovation, you're enjoying the response while gearing up for the question-and-answer session.

At the appropriate time, you'll reflect on how you could have improved your introduction. You ended up doing well in your presentation, but for next time, you'll have to start doing better sooner.

BIG IMPACT OPENINGS

There are a number of ways of creating some major bonding moments with the audience out of the gate. They're based on the fact that listeners (most of them, at least) love to be acknowledged.

If you have the financial resources, and it's appropriate to the event, you could assume the role of a reporter the day before your presentation and, with a professional videographer in tow, humorously interview delegates on conference-themed subjects.

You'd then have the videographer edit the interview clips into an entertaining "news story," under your talented direction.

Upon taking the lectern the next day to deliver your presentation, you'd introduce the story with the appropriate measure of theatrics.

The "news story" invariably goes down exceptionally well.

Of course, you could always conduct, tape, and edit the interviews yourself, but the results run the risk of being uneven at best. If you're looking to make an impression with an important audience, play it safe and hire a professional.

Really making it about the audience

If you don't have the resources or the time to pull off the reporter gambit, and you have a relationship with a special individual attending the conference, you can always take a more conventional, but still effective route.

The person could be a beloved manager about to retire (dear old Sadie) or a volunteer firefighter who's recently saved a child (stand-up Cyril.) Whoever it is, you want to make sure that the audience will look favourably upon their recognition.

Now, order a professional sports jersey with the honoree's last name on the back (just like the athletes have), and present it with feeling.

Celebrating Sadie

Here's an example of how this mini-presentation might go:

> I'd like to acknowledge a special member of our audience. Sadie Anderson has been with our organization for thirty-one years, and will be retiring next month. Sadie, you've made a tremendous contribution to the company, in many ways. You've certainly helped me become a better leader, and I'll always be grateful for your counsel and your kindness.
>
> I think everyone in this room knows that Sadie is a huge fan of the Toronto Maple Leafs. She not only took me under her wing when I joined the company, she cheers for the Leafs — Sadie clearly loves a challenge.
>
> Sadie, as an expression of our respect and affection, and to ensure you're well outfitted when watching your beloved team, please accept this Maple Leafs jersey, featuring your name and the number thirty-one to mark the number of years you've contributed to the success of our company.
>
> Thank you, Sadie. You're the best.

The presentation to Sadie (or whoever the honoree might be) accomplishes several important goals.

It warms the crowd like few overtures can, gets your listeners involved from the outset as they celebrate Sadie, and communicates the fact that you're someone who's willing to share the spotlight.

Remember: the more power you give away, the more power comes back to you.

An important caution here. Always have a back-up plan.

There's the chance that Sadie might not make it to the conference, or your speech, for whatever reason. Make sure to have another honouree waiting in the wings. Perhaps it's Cyril, the firefighter hero. If both attend, you'd present a jersey to each, for maximum impact.

Two honorees can make for just as big an impact as one, but three never can. It's just too many. This is one of the few times when the Power of Three doesn't apply.

"You" works better than "I"

Throughout your presentation, you found that some words worked exceptionally well, and some, not so much.

One of the words that worked spectacularly well was "you" — as in the members of your audience. Whenever you said "you," your listeners appeared to pay special attention.

Why? It's because the information to come was going to be about them.

President Obama understands the power of the word "you." He employs it frequently. In doing so, he makes the members of his audience feel valued, included. Important.

In his acceptance speech at the Democratic National Convention in Denver in August 2008, Obama told his enraptured supporters, "What the naysayers don't understand is that this election has never been about me. It's about you."

It's a matter of respect for your listeners. For speakers, the benefits of that form of engagement can be extraordinary. It's something to think about as you consider the presentation you've just given, and all the presentations to come.

THE EYES HAVE IT

As you reflect on what worked — and what didn't — in your keynote, there's one major finding that didn't come as a surprise.

And that's the power of eye contact.

An enormous and often underemphasized part of communication, eye contact binds speakers with their audiences, teachers with their students, and parents with their children.

With it, we feel engaged. Without it, we feel disconnected.

Perhaps you've witnessed this for yourself. Take, for example, the president of an organization in your sector as he was making an impassioned point at his company's annual meeting.

As he was concluding his thought, he became concerned with the next part of his script. As a result, he looked down at his notes and away from the audience. Things declined from there.

The president's voice, strong and certain in the early part of his presentation, softened and tailed off as he lost the critical visual relationship with the crowd.

The audience needs it

Listeners grew confused — here was an important point, everyone knew that, so why wasn't the company leader driving it home with eye contact?

"Why," the members of the audience were mentally asking the president, "aren't you looking at us?"

If you and I are conversing and you're not looking at me, I won't believe you. I *can't* believe you.

If we're talking and you look over my shoulder to spot someone more powerful (which is just about everyone) or more interesting (which *is* everyone) I'll be offended, perhaps not forever, but I'll certainly remember your discourtesy for as long.

To communicate convincingly, we all need to master the art of eye contact.

Big-ticket speakers who make the equivalent of a middle manager's annual salary with a single address, headliners such as Bill Clinton, utilize visual connectivity like a marvelously tuned instrument. They know that without it, even the best oratory will go flat.

We can learn from the pros. We can learn how to direct and calibrate eye contact to fully engage our audiences and bring our message to life.

Here's how.

Use it early

You know that the first ninety seconds of a presentation are crucial. Lose the crowd here and you may as well screen an episode of *Mad Men*.

You also know that committing the first minute and a half of your narrative to memory pays significant dividends, enabling you to focus on establishing a strong visual rapport with the audience. Once it's been established, you can look down at your script or notes more often if you need to, and your listeners won't resent it (at least not as much as if you've started off the presentation that way).

You need to bookend your presentation with terrific eye contact. Remember, start and end with impact.

Make it personal

You can cut a large audience down to a psychologically manageable size. Select three or four friendly, supportive listeners in different parts of the room and pay special attention to them.

In smaller groups, always make sure that you engage the most senior person at the table, the ultimate decision-maker.

Make every line credible

Regardless of how well you know your stuff, you need to start and conclude each sentence with eye contact — it's your ongoing link with the audience.

While it's acceptable, indeed natural, to occasionally look down or away in the middle of a line, if you do it at the beginning or the end, listeners won't buy what you're selling.

Accomplished speakers can begin a line without eye contact, often dramatically, but for most presenters it's far better to play it safe. The risks of losing your connection with your listeners — of not fully engaging them — far outweigh the potential rewards.

Make it a rule to begin and end each sentence with eye contact.

Take a break

While it's essential for a great presentation, speakers who maintain unbroken eye contact with their audience can be downright creepy.

Real people involved in authentic human discourse do occasionally look away from those they're addressing. It's absolutely fine, as long as you do it at the right times.

And when you do it, look down, which appears thoughtful, not up, which can seem disingenuous.

Your best lines need it

You know that in any presentation you'll have key content that needs to be conveyed with special emphasis. You also know that you'll need to calibrate the volume and inflection of your voice to hammer your best points home.

However, if you haven't infused your language with the authority of eye contact, you really won't have fully engaged your audience. You'll have missed the mark.

You see, the eyes have it.

REPETITION RULES

Public speaking always involves a few surprises.

There are lines that work, phrases that don't, and those times when your material resonates so well you're taken by surprise.

You attained that agreeable circumstance in your keynote when you employed repetition.

Repetition rules. It's a tremendous way of engaging your listeners.

A frequent deficiency of contemporary speeches and presentations is that they're written as if an audience will be reading, rather than hearing, them.

President Obama certainly understands the need for auditory impact. He's re-introduced the practice of repetition, which had largely disappeared from oratory, as if speakers somehow believed that repeating a key word or phrase made them appear less than erudite.

In reality, the opposite is true.

Listeners welcome repetition because it clarifies a message; it lets them know what you, as a speaker, consider important.

It also indicates that you're passionate and confident enough in your message to emphasize it in a way that will stick with audiences.

Consider Mr. Obama's repetition of the word "need" during a speech on responsibility in Chicago in June 2008, when he was a candidate for the Democratic Party's presidential nomination.

"We also need families to raise our children. We

need fathers to realize that responsibility does not end at conception. We need them to realize that what makes you a man is not the ability to have a child — it's the courage to raise one."

Spoken by a Yankee immortal

Speakers have long recognized the strength of repetition.

Consider the repetitive use of the word "when" by New York Yankees great Lou Gehrig, stricken with ALS, Amyotrophic Lateral Sclerosis, in his historic farewell address at Yankee Stadium on July 4, 1939:

> When the New York Giants, a team you would give your right arm to beat, and vice versa, sends you a gift — that's something.
>
> When everybody down to the groundskeepers and those boys in white coats remember you with trophies — that's something.
>
> When you have a wonderful mother-in-law who takes sides with you in squabbles with her own daughter — that's something.
>
> When you have a father and a mother who work all their lives so you can have an education and build your body — it's a blessing.
>
> When you have a wife who has been a tower of strength and shown more courage than you dreamed existed — that's the finest I know.

A prime minister employed it

In his farewell speech at the Liberal Leadership Convention in June 1984, Prime Minister Pierre Trudeau said, "Whenever the going was tough and we were opposed by the multinationals, or by the provincial premiers, or by the superpowers — I realized that if our cause was right, all we had to do to win was to talk over the heads of the premiers, over the heads of the multinationals, over the heads of the superpowers to the people of this land, to the people of Canada!"

Repetition has worked for generations. It works today.

You found that out for yourself when, in your presentation, you delivered three sharp lines to emphasize your company's position on partnerships. You said:

> We're looking for the right markets — not any market.
>
> We're looking for the right deals — not any deal.
>
> We're looking for the right partners — not any partner.

You spoke those lines slowly, emphatically and convincingly, and your listeners were receptive.

When English is your second language

When solidly constructed and well expressed, repetition can raise the game of any speaker. It's an especially valuable option for those who speak English as a second language.

In predominantly English-speaking countries, they face added pressure in the workplace. It comes from being judged on how well they converse in the world's dominant business tongue by clients, colleagues, and bosses who may have spoken it since childhood.

If those who speak English as a second language fall short of the standards set by others, their careers can get stuck, or knocked off the rails altogether.

You may be the smartest person in the room, with the best credentials to boot, but if your audience can't understand you — or gets frustrated and distracted attempting to comprehend what you're trying to say — all your abilities may be undermined.

Verbal skills need to be a career asset, not a liability.

If English is your second language, how do you address others effectively, particularly when there's a ton on the line in a big presentation?

Here are some principles to follow.

Keep it uncomplicated

Of course you need to master the fundamental vocabulary of a language to be able to communicate persuasively in it. But even after you've achieved a respectable level of knowledge, you should always aim for simplicity.

By far, the most common mistake those speaking English as a second language make is to overextend themselves, to become too ambitious in their selection of words and phrases. They can undermine their confidence and lose credibility by stumbling over a narrative that's unnecessarily complicated.

You don't win many points for pronouncing intricate words with precision, but you can lose a lot by failing to deliver them cleanly. After all, they're your words. You picked them.

Why risk it? Keep it simple.

Establish yourself

If your listeners don't know you well, you need to relate your position, experience, and credentials right out of the gate.

Audiences have a tendency to subconsciously discount the experiences of those who don't share the same background. It isn't necessarily malicious; it's human nature.

Make sure those you're addressing have the contextual information to fully understand who you are and what you're able to bring to the table — your skills, accomplishments, and commitment.

Embrace your accent

It's extraordinarily difficult for adults raised in another language to eradicate an accent in order to communicate flawlessly in English. Many tie themselves into knots trying to do it.

Your accent is part of you. Certainly, you can lessen it with practice and time, but the goal shouldn't be to sound like everybody else. Your goal should be to sound like you, accent or not, speaking English clearly and simply, in a way that listeners can easily understand.

Go slowly

We've learned about the advantages of speaking slowly, particularly in the early going of a presentation. When English is your second language, it's especially important to begin slowly. Listeners need time to adapt to your accent, even if it's slight, and get used to an intonation that may require greater concentration.

Proceeding slowly also helps you with difficult-to-pronounce technical and financial terms, giving you time to break them down and say them carefully.

It's far better to be measured and right than fast and wrong.

Deliver solid lines — repeat

We know the best presentations are marked by short, crisp, well-delivered statements that stand out due to their clarity and punch.

Produce a simple thematic line that you can articulate smoothly and convey with authority.

It could be, "It's all about innovation."

Now, repeat that line several times during your presentation. It will infuse some energy into your words, and demonstrate that you're confident enough in your message to employ repetition to convey it.

Stay positive

Those who speak English as a second language can be awfully hard on themselves, self-critical and apologetic when their diction isn't spot on.

Once you reach a certain level of linguistic competence, through study and practice, you need never apologize.

So stay positive. And remember that when speakers

are prepared and committed, listeners for the most part are tremendously supportive — in English or in any other language.

THE GIVE AND TAKE OF FEEDBACK

Much of what you did in your presentation worked splendidly — some of it, not so much.

You'll be pleased that you had your speech digitally recorded. As a result, you'll be able to watch it later and see for yourself what elements of your content and delivery require improvement.

My advice: when you do watch it, be rested, relaxed, and in good spirits.

Some presenters prefer to view themselves in privacy, since it can be a disconcerting experience to assume the role of an audience member as you watch yourself, every physical and verbal flaw exposed.

Disconcerting, but compulsory, if you want to improve.

I continue to be perplexed by executives who speak poorly in public, and often have for many years, yet never take any action to get better.

They lack not only the initiative to improve, but even the interest in hearing an objective opinion of how they address others. All they're interested in hearing is, "That was great."

Doing tough self-analysis and soliciting feedback,

whatever it entails, is an essential step in becoming a better presenter. Without it, you won't be speaking like a leader any time soon.

Deliver it with care, accept it with appreciation

Feedback should always be accepted for what it is — a gift. Too often, though, it's deployed as a weapon.

That's because feedback, the stated perception or evaluation of one's conduct or performance, is rarely delivered with the care and introspection with which it's received. When it's conveyed poorly, and far too often it is, feedback creates wounds, resentments, and muted loyalty.

Badly expressed feedback makes for bad business.

In today's corporate world, there's a tendency to regard colleagues and employees as replaceable engine parts rather than enormously complex, sensitive beings who carry around with them decades of emotional experience. Be sensitive to their needs, even if you don't know the details of their backgrounds.

Generations come and go, but this truth endures and always will: people crave self-esteem. They want to be recognized as being important and valuable.

In this area at least there's no difference between the sullen teenage skateboarder with his nose ring and the fastidious, pinstriped senior executive with her new, designer briefcase.

They're both saying to the world, "Hey, look at me, I matter!"

They both matter. We all matter. Yet despite that basic realization, we're often challenged to provide decent, non-confrontational, affirming assessment and advice.

The fumbling of feedback goes both ways. On the receiving end we're often far too fragile, folding into our reaction a host of insecurities and grievances unrelated and unhelpful to the situation at hand. The criticism of an element of your work isn't an assault upon your worth as a human being.

The commitment to providing thoughtful, well-balanced feedback — and to receiving it in a mature manner — enhances relationships and organizations.

Here are four guidelines on feedback to keep in mind.

Accept negative feedback calmly

When receiving negative feedback, separate "you" the executive from "you" the human being. Resist the impulse to make it personal. Breathe deeply. Stay calm and focused.

Ask questions to clarify observations, "I understand your concern. How do you think I might have introduced the topic in a better way? How would you have done it?"

If you feel the evaluation is unfair or biased, buy time in order to respond rationally and professionally. "I'd like to think about that for a bit. May we pick this conversation up later?"

Above all, consider the benefit that is feedback. Someone, presumably a colleague you respect, has expended the resources of time and energy to share insights that, when processed constructively, will benefit your career.

As the comedian David Spade might say, "And the problem with that would be…?"

Provide negative feedback with sensitivity

Be direct when dealing out feedback. But be sensitive, too. If you require inspiration, think about your worst experience on the blunt end of criticism.

Keep in mind that as a leader, you should be delivering more complimentary feedback than negative.

There's a well-accepted rule in communication skills coaching that dictates the facilitator render two positive, legitimate comments about a participant's performance before every critical one. Manipulation? Hardly. It's a matter of balance. Those on the receiving end of the commentary need to feel a degree of comfort in their relationship with the evaluator, or they simply shut down.

However, don't overdo the affirmations and leave a piece of critical, negative-based feedback to the end — the recipient really *will* feel manipulated.

Give it in person, promptly

The recipients of feedback, especially when it's negative, deserve to hear it from you in person, and if that's not possible, over the phone.

They also deserve to hear it as soon as possible, not five months down the line at their annual review.

Any delay will deprive your colleagues of knowledge that might benefit them immediately. If you hold off too long they'll also resent you for all the time you knew (or felt) something they didn't know.

Keep an open mind

If you're passing on feedback that's come from others, information you didn't glean from your own observations, tread carefully.

You may not know (or have been told) the whole story. Others may have less than altruistic agendas. Give the affected parties plenty of time and opportunity to provide their interpretation of events.

Of course, not all feedback features unfavourable evaluations.

When you're on the receiving end of a positive appraisal, enjoy it. Don't blow if off by responding, "It was nothing" or "Anyone could have done it."

Instead, smile, make firm eye contact with your reviewer and say, "Thank you!"

Accept the gift.

DEALING WITH DIFFICULT PEOPLE

You were fortunate in your presentation — no difficult audience members.

Sure, a few listeners were chatting animatedly away as you commenced your remarks, but they soon stopped.

They'd become compelled by your story. That's a testament to how well you prepared, and how effectively you engaged your audience. You didn't get distracted or distressed by the tiny minority who demonstrated a deficit of manners. You kept your cool, and your focus.

The inconsiderate and rude abound these days. They exhibit a host of infuriating behaviours — among them yakking loudly and obliviously on cellphones in public places, blocking traffic after blithely driving into congested intersections at the turn of a light, and, incomprehensively, walking smack into you on city sidewalks.

Is the long-established pedestrian directive of bearing to one's right so difficult to follow?

Sadly, the number of obnoxious among us appears to be increasing exponentially.

It's a statistical certainty that if you deliver enough presentations, conduct enough workshops, and run enough meetings, you'll eventually encounter members of this disagreeable crew.

They're easily identified under two main personality types: the know-it-all and the disrupter.

The good news is that members of both groups can be successfully managed. It's a matter of taking them on early and decisively. If you don't, they'll weaken your authority while traumatizing your audience.

Let's examine how to handle those who seek to undermine our communication, according to their disorder.

The know-it-all

He thinks he knows everything. And he's obsessed with convincing everyone else that he does, in fact, know everything.

In a Q & A, he'll go on at some length about his background, experience, and achievements before posing a question. It will become apparent from his tone, and his inevitable follow-up query, that he considers your knowledge and abilities inferior.

If you're running a workshop, he'll interrupt you early and often. He'll look for contradictions and inconsistencies, and insist on providing the group with his commentary, relevant or not.

A know-it-all identifies himself even before a meeting begins. He'll strut in with a swagger and a slight roll of the eyes, and invariably position himself as far away from other participants as possible. (Why would he sit with them when he's so much smarter?)

Then the challenges begin.

You need to deal with difficult personality types through escalating stages of response.

For the know-it-all, the first stage is engagement. Ask him his first name. Use it frequently in conversation; his ears will prick up at the sound.

Ask him questions: "Bob, what's your experience been in that area?"

Your intention is to make the know-it-all an ally, a co-presenter, a supporter.

Certainly, you'll pay a price at the outset, because Bob will undoubtedly take up a lot of the proceedings.

But far better to have him contribute positively. After he's had his status as the brightest entity in the Free World confirmed, you can back off and begin paying more attention to the other participants. In rare cases, Bob won't respond to your outreach. He'll continue to confront you, immobilizing your session and irritating other participants.

Now, it's time to get tough.

Stage two has to do with reminding the know-it-all (and, therefore, the group) of your expertise, while noting the limitations of his.

If Bob still doesn't play ball, it's time to deploy the heavy artillery. Freeze him out. Limit eye contact with him. Answer his questions quickly and succinctly, continually reminding the group (and, therefore, Bob) that you have a busy agenda to get through.

In the vast majority of cases, the know-it-all will begin to exhibit the type of responsible conduct that facilitates re-entry. But remember: never gloat. And when facing defiance, never panic. Always keep your communication cool.

The disrupter

The disrupter likes to talk, which can be a problem, because he often insists on doing so during presentations. When speaking to a large group, you almost always have to ignore him. In a smaller group meeting, you need to take him on.

There's another kind of disrupter, represented by those angry and distraught individuals who vent their collective rage in public information meetings organized to brief them on some government proposal or decision, perhaps having to do with a local concern.

Of course, in our democracy, the right to publicly express our opinions doesn't — and shouldn't — extend to tromping on the rights of others to express theirs.

Public officials at every level have set a bad precedent in public meetings, which have been set up ostensibly for the respectful exchange of information and views. They'll sit at the front of an auditorium, allowing themselves to be interrupted, insulted, and occasionally threatened by hundreds of enraged listeners. Nothing good or productive ever comes out of these encounters.

The officials have rights, too. For starters, they have the right not to be verbally abused or intimidated.

However, they often make it tougher on themselves by failing to set the ground rules for audience conduct; they need to state up front that profanity, insults, and shouting won't be tolerated. Swear once, and you're warned. Swear twice and you're asked to leave. Refuse to leave and security gets called. Everyone pretty much gets the drill after that.

Placating the difficult among us may work for a time. But like the schoolyard bullies of our youth, they need to be confronted.

In communication, as in life, the sooner you do it, the better.

THE QUESTION-AND-ANSWER SESSION

It's time for your Q & A session.

You set yourself up well for the Q & A by ending your presentation with impact, and leaving plenty of time — eight to ten seconds, for instance — between the last words of your address and your invitation to the audience to ask questions.

A lot of speakers aren't as poised.

They'll conclude their remarks with a "thank you," followed immediately by, "I'll now be happy to take any questions." They don't give the audience an opportunity to respond with a full round of applause.

Leaders take their time. This is a perfect example of when being in the moment enhances your relationship with listeners and communicates the fact you're self-assured and in control.

Sometimes, following a presentation, a moderator will be on hand to thank you for your remarks and solicit questions from the crowd.

But frequently, you'll have to manage the exercise on your own.

However it's initiated, a question-and-answer session separates the leaders from the posers. Few career-related skills are more impressive than the ability to respond to questions — even loaded, hostile, circuitous questions — with tangible confidence and insightful analysis.

Play twenty questions

That ability doesn't come without preparation.

Plan for the Q & A well in advance by compiling a list of the twenty questions that could most likely be asked of you. Rehearse your responses to those questions — coolly and cordially — and you'll be well on your way.

Consider those questions, any questions really, to represent yet another way for you to tell your story and, by extension, expand your influence.

More than a few presenters get intimidated by the Q & A, fearful that they won't be able to answer every query brilliantly.

It's the wrong thought process.

No one knows everything.

In the unlikely event you're baffled by a question, you can simply say, "I don't know."

If you're committed to finding the answer, you can add, "I'll be pleased to find out and contact you with the information," or you can poll the audience to determine if anyone else knows the answer.

Far from reducing your credibility, you'll be building it up. Assuming you've established your expertise and credentials during your presentation, the audience will be impressed that you have the confidence and integrity to acknowledge what you don't know.

The worst tact you can take is to guess, pontificate, or dissemble. You'll come across as insecure and insincere.

When the questions don't come

We've all experienced those awkward seconds when nothing but quiet — and a few nervous coughs — greets the invitation, "Now, our distinguished speaker will be pleased to answer a few questions."

With any luck, following a painful interlude of silence the moderator of your event won't say, "Well, I guess your presentation was so well done that it answered everybody's questions!"

At the outset, if there are no questions from the audience, ask a question of yourself to kick the session off.

"You know, the question I'm most often asked by people in our industry is ..." and away you go.

Asking and answering the first question usually opens up a stream of queries from the floor. However, if there are still no questions after you've initiated and handled the first one, ask yourself a second question and answer it.

If there are still no questions from your listeners, shut the session down.

"Thank you, everyone, for the privilege of speaking with you today."

To excel in the Q & A, revisit your presentation

Experienced speakers rarely get stumped in a Q & A. That's because 90 percent of their responses can be found in the material they've just covered in their presentations.

It's simply a matter of making the link. Here's an example:

Question: "Why do you think so many companies have trouble determining and articulating a clear vision?"

Answer: "It's a question a lot of people are asking. In my presentation, I made the point that a company needs to express its vision with a unified voice. Within any large, complex organization there are a lot of opinions fighting to be heard on the subject of vision, so there's often a great deal of confusion about where the outfit is heading — and why. It's the CEO's job to determine a clear, coherent vision, and communicate it to the world. Unfortunately, many CEOs don't, won't, or can't do it."

A lot of communication consultants advise speakers not to say "great question" in response to a query that's especially clever or thoughtful, but I don't mind this phrase — after all, some questions are better than others, and you want to be real.

However, I wouldn't use the expression more than once during a single Q & A session. If you've already reached your quota and you get another outstanding question, you could say, "That's another excellent question."

People ask questions for a variety of reasons: to be recognized for how smart they are, to issue a challenge, or simply because they're genuinely interested in your response.

Regardless of motivation, every questioner needs to be treated with respect.

When a member of the audience is treated too casually or cavalierly, every listener feels it — even if the questioner being blown off doesn't reflect the group's sensibilities.

The respect factor

A fascinating psychology emerges during presentations and Q & A sessions. Audience members may have few common interests, but they'll nevertheless bond with one another.

Being part of an audience with a troublesome member is much like being part of a large family with a wacky uncle. Your uncle may drink like a fish, borrow money he never repays, and embarrass you at barbeques, but he's still a member of the family.

He doesn't deserve to be put down or disrespected in public.

It takes a lot for the members of an audience to censure one of their own. Crimes qualifying for denunciation include talking incessantly during presentations, using profanity, and threatening or engaging in violence.

A listener almost has to try to get thrown out of the club.

As a speaker, you have a much more narrow road to navigate. That's why it's so important to treat every audience member with courtesy.

Q & A choreography

Make polite, non-combative eye contact with each questioner, even the difficult questioner, and try never to interrupt when a question is being asked — even if it's lengthy, confusing, or nonsensical.

Once it's been posed, you can seek clarification, or you can repeat the query, receiving the questioner's approval of its accuracy, as you relate it to the group.

"This gentleman was asking my opinion of the most recent federal government report on the future of our industry, and why we should care. Do I have that right, sir?"

When a question is being asked, look at the questioner.

When you're repeating the question for the sake of clarity, or so every listener in the room can hear it, pull your eyes away from the questioner to address the audience as a whole. As you're concluding your response, return to the questioner and say, "Thank you."

I'm relentlessly risk-averse when it comes to presentations and Q & A, so I'll never ask, "Did that answer your question?"

What if the person says no?

That would be a drag, and potentially place a damper on the entire proceedings.

Usually the questioner is happy with the response. If not, he'll often have a follow-up question.

It's then up to you to decide whether to take the question, or offer to discuss the issue with him after the session in person, in a telephone call, or by email.

Please, whatever you do, don't say, "Can we take this offline?"

It's become a dreadful, meaningless cliché, right down there with win-win, strategic alignment, and collaborative consultation.

When the going gets rough

For hostile questions, remain calm and listen attentively. Restate the question as positively as possible, and respond with your experience, evidence, or reputable third-party support or endorsement.

It's fine to disagree with a questioner. But you should always aim to find at least some common ground, so you can conclude the interaction on an upbeat or at least a neutral note.

Here's a hostile question, with a possible response.

Question: "You were making a big deal in your speech about your recent 'loyalty' sales initiative. Well, my company tried the same thing and it went nowhere. Isn't this just a lot of hype?"

Whatever you do, don't repeat the negative and say, "It's not a lot of hype." Speak in positives.

Answer: "Our initiative generated significant results. As I indicated in my presentation, our sales for the third quarter were up 17 percent, and that was due primarily to the program. It just goes to show that two organizations can have entirely different results with a 'loyalty' sales undertaking. I will say this — to be successful, it requires a ton of resources and significant commitment from upper management. I'd welcome the chance to learn more about your company's experience after the meeting."

Think of yourself as the host at a big gathering. You're responsible for making sure everyone feels welcomed, valued, and informed.

Nothing is a problem for you. You can deal adroitly with any challenge, any awkwardness, any silence. Anything.

You're a pro, a leader.

And this is how leaders speak.

Ten Tips for the Q & A Session

1. List and rehearse your responses to the twenty questions most likely to be asked of you.
2. Leave enough time between the end of your presentation and the start of the Q & A for the audience to acknowledge you.
3. If no one has asked a question at the outset, ask and answer your own.
4. Consider questions just another opportunity to tell your story.
5. Never guess, pontificate, or dissemble.
6. Treat all questioners, even difficult ones, with courtesy and respect.
7. Don't be afraid to say, "I don't know."
8. Stay in your communication "box."
9. Employ transitions to bridge back to your story.
10. Aim to end every response on an upbeat or at least a neutral note.

Think "inside" the box

When dealing with questions from the audience, mundane and aggressive alike, utilize a concept that skilled media spokespersons employ and stay in your communication "box."

Think of the box as a container of information, a place from which we convey news and perspectives as we speak with others. It's safe and secure inside the box, because we're invariably confident in the material it holds, and practised in communicating the contents.

What goes in the box?

It's simple: your story, information to support it, and transition or bridging phrases that enable you to smoothly return to it when questioners challenge your account, or attempt to lead you from it.

"Let's get back to the central issue," is an example of a transition or bridging statement.

There's no more valuable item in our language toolbox than the transition, which can smoothly convey conversationalists out of potentially damaging exchanges and into verbal safe houses, where they can quickly regroup and respond.

Although transitions are often overlooked in communication, they're essential to effective discourse. They alter the condition of dialogue and provide us with an invaluable link to our story, where we can focus — and have others focus — on the issues we choose to emphasize.

Transitions have gotten a bad rap, mainly because they've been overused — and misused — by spin doctors and those they advise.

But a transition isn't meant to obfuscate; it's meant to facilitate.

For communication to serve us well, we need to supply it with limits: limits of time, limits of appropriateness, and limits of subject matter. For example, we'd never speak about the strategy of an organization, including our own, unless we were absolutely certain of what it was. If we didn't know definitively, we'd be departing our communication box, risking the erosion of our credibility for negligible advantage.

If transitions didn't exist, no one in conversation would ever get to tell their story, so fraught would their narrative be with disparate responses to the questions and challenges of others.

The tale of a transition

But there's a big caveat here: a transition needs to be rational and sensibly integrated. If it's unrelated to the conversation at hand, combative, or inane, the transition itself becomes the take-away message, rather than a well-accepted conduit to the story.

Lifestyle guru Martha Stewart found that out during a television appearance in June 2002. Appearing on the CBS *The Early Show* to chat about summer recipes, Stewart was asked about the investigation into her sale in late 2001 of nearly four thousand shares of the biotech company ImClone Systems, a transaction that, as it turned out, violated insider trading laws and was ultimately responsible for sending her to prison.

"This will all be resolved in the very near future," Stewart told host Jayne Clayson, "and I will be exonerated of any ridiculousness." She reasoned that she would continue on with her business.

Then came her memorable words: "I want to focus on my salad, because that's why I'm here."

Almost immediately, the media began feasting on Stewart's delicious salad quote. It led virtually every news report about her television appearance, and continues to rank as one of the most amusing transitions of the new century.

It's a natural reaction to respond defensively when we're under verbal attack, or even pressure. It's natural, but rarely effective, and provides the assault with a perverse credibility.

The best communicators know that in professional interactions — such as a Q & A session, a company meeting, or a media interview — they're best served by a calm, well-considered transition.

Top Ten Transitions

1. "I see things differently."(Respectful, but firm.)
2. "On the contrary" or "just the opposite"(Quickly re-orients the conversation without restating the negative.)
3. "That's not the issue. The issue is ..." (Strong, forceful.)
4. "Let me provide some background." (Needed perspective, your way.)
5. "That would be speculation. What I can confirm

is that ..." (You can only speak about what you know.)

6. "The important point here is that ..." (Difficult to ignore.)

7. "That's true. However, what you need to consider is ..." (Polite perspective.)

8. "I don't know. I'll be pleased to find out and contact you with the information. What I do know is that ..." (Make sure what you say now has real value.)

9. "Let's get back to the central issue." (Confident re-direct.)

10. "I'd like to emphasize ..." (To solidify your point.)

The Fifth Key — Commitment

You've worked hard and spoken admirably.

Your CEO is delighted.

Your colleagues are impressed. Shortly after your presentation, Peggy spoke with Tim, as he was departing Berlin for Vegas. He's just sent you a congratulatory email (it appears you have a new "best office friend").

Most importantly, you served your audience conscientiously.

Your professional standing has been enhanced by your contribution to "Industry 2020," and you deserve to celebrate tonight.

AN EXHILARATING JOURNEY FOR YOUNG AND OLD

You've embarked on a marvelous quest, to speak consistently like a leader.

It will require more than you giving the occasional presentation at an industry conference; it demands that you communicate with excellence in every situation imaginable, whether the audience consists of one or one thousand.

Most of us have the wherewithal to achieve that goal. You can be young, old, or middle-aged. It doesn't matter.

You can start speaking like a leader in the workplace.

Today, the members of four generations often work side-by-side, frequently under the financial stress brought about by the Great Recession. All of us bring the values and experiences common to our age group into our correspondence, conversations, and presentations. If we don't grasp or, at the very least, respect the perspective of our audiences from different generations, we run the risk of creating misunderstanding and resentment.

Intergenerational communication can be tough, whether it's going up or down the chronological chain.

Let's examine the challenges from two outlooks, the younger worker and the older employee, and discover how each can engage and inspire their opposite-age audiences.

For the young business professional

You look like you're still in high school, and when you interact with older colleagues at the office, you usually feel like it. You perceive that, despite your obvious intellect and accomplishments, more senior listeners don't take you seriously. There's an apparent lack of attention and, perhaps, even respect.

Indeed, there's danger of a communication breakdown.

As a younger employee, you have more to lose if that happens, given the standard age-related distribution of power — more age, more authority — in the workplace.

But you never have to lose if you follow these simple rules for communicating effectively with older colleagues.

Consider your audience

Your baby boomer parents think you're fabulous; the curmudgeon in the corner office may not.

Younger employees are often their own worst enemies when interacting with more senior co-workers, engaging them as if they were weekend party chums rather than professional associates.

Inappropriate familiarity will undermine your relationships with many older executives, managers, and even peers who came up the ranks when business was more hierarchal and business conduct was more reserved, at least outwardly.

So, err on the side of formality when first meeting more senior personnel. For example, "It's a pleasure to meet you, Mr. Smith," rather than "It's amazing to connect, Ed."

Mr. Smith will let you know if he wants you to call him by his first name, or not.

Then, listen more than you speak. In fact, the younger you are, the more you should listen. You'll learn things.

Understand your audience

The more you know about others, the better you can relate to them.

Chances are that at least some of your senior associates once worked in offices when there were typewriters instead of computers, the mere description of email would have been considered fantasy, and the only place women were seen was in the secretarial pool.

That may seem like a long time ago. It wasn't, really. Make sure to keep that in mind when communicating with the older generation.

Be strategic

Of course, you can still be "you." But be you in a way that enhances, rather than hurts, your prospects.

In new interactions with older executives who aren't familiar with your background, refer early on to your work-related credentials and experience, then let those colleagues take the conversational lead.

Resist the urge to share your mesmerizing snowboarding stories until a solid relationship has been established, and ask thoughtful, specific questions.

Mine the brains of older co-workers for their knowledge and advice. Everyone likes to be asked his or her opinion. You'll benefit from a variety of viewpoints, and be remembered.

Dress like a leader

It's a cliché, but more true now than ever: if you look like a kid and dress like a kid, you shouldn't be surprised — or offended — if you're treated like one.

Never underestimate the influence of quality apparel; it represents a huge opportunity for younger employees looking to make their mark.

As office attire becomes increasingly casual, you can stand out from the pedestrian crowd by wearing a fashionable, pinstriped suit. It doesn't have to be expensive, but it does have to fit impeccably. Colleagues, including those of the more senior variety, are sure to notice. And you'll feel your confidence soar.

True, some members of your office crew may consider you a sellout for dressing so stylishly. That's too bad. You're a grown up now. You have a career. And this is all about taking every opportunity to build it.

There's an old saying in business: When you're selling, dress up. When you're buying, dress down.

When you're in the working world, you're continually selling a product — yourself — whether you acknowledge it or not. The younger you are when you accept that fact, the better off you'll be.

Speak like you're older

Certain words and phrases routinely employed by younger employees grate on the nerves of older colleagues.

"You guys" is especially loathed. Then there's "like" (as in, "like, I wrecked the hybrid"), "totally," and "cool," which is a great word except when it's pronounced, as the young so often do, "kewl."

Of course, the young don't have a monopoly on the use of irritating language, but they seem to dominate the aggravating habit of inflecting up at the end of sentences, as if they're perpetually asking a question (as in, "like, I babysat last night?").

If you want to communicate persuasively with older listeners, keep your narrative free of the terminologies that are sure to raise their collective blood pressure, and inflect down at the end of your sentences.

For the middle-aged workplace veteran

You're still sharp, still happening, still on top of your game.

It's too bad your younger colleagues — the "kids" — might not believe it.

They marginalize you, or at least you think they do, often dismissing you as overbearing, dated, and narrow. You consider that treatment disrespectful and inaccurate, since you could save your younger associates a lot of time and anguish if they'd just defer to your knowledge and acumen in the first place.

Welcome to the confounding world of intergenerational relationships.

It's an environment that can be especially baffling for more senior employees, many of whom learned how to interact with professional colleagues of varying demographics when the rules of engagement were much clearer.

There was a formula then. Your seniority — defined by your age and level within an organization — determined how much you could say and to whom you could say it. Today, there's a far more subtle, much less rigid system of dialogue in place.

So how can you, an older worker, communicate effectively with your younger colleagues? Here are some guidelines.

Ditch the self-obsession

You were at Woodstock in 1969. That's terrific. However, that long-ago adventure shouldn't form the core of your ongoing narrative.

A common criticism of older employees — especially those enchanting baby boomers — is that they often talk about their experiences, personal and professional, as if they were somehow transcendent, superior to all experiences before or since.

While the members of previous generations won wars, returned home, spoke little of their heroics, and built families and businesses, the boomers have loudly broadcast every mundane activity along the way ("Look, I'm jogging!").

To connect with younger associates, older employees need to relinquish the notion that their pasts are inherently richer than the shorter histories of their colleagues. Your escapades weren't necessarily more fun, your parties hotter, or your degree tougher to earn. With age should come respect, but not if you abuse the rank.

Be fully engaged

You've been at your game a long time, but not so long that you can't learn anything new. Let your younger compatriots know that. Ask questions of junior associates like they matter, and that their knowledge and opinions count for something.

The older you are, the more power you wield, and the more of an interest you take in others, the more impressive the effect.

The payoff? You'll discover things. For one, you'll get the perspective of astute members of a different generation, which can't help but enhance your later-career intelligence.

Embrace your age

You were young once. Now, you're not, so please don't speak in the hip, urban lexicon of those significantly younger — unless you're intent on appearing down-right pitiable.

That means eliminating the following phrases from your vocabulary: "I dig it," "I'm down with that," and "I got totally wasted last night."

Oh, and a point on attire. Leave those much-too-tight jeans in the "not for work" section of the closest.

Be fit

If younger employees underestimate the credibility-enhancing influence of quality clothing in the office, then senior workers often don't get the age-mitigating power of fitness.

Older, fit executives communicate self-discipline and vitality; their corpulent colleagues convey self-indulgence and the overwhelming need for a nap.

We live in a world of perfection-based images that have raised the bar for attractiveness and vitality. In the workplace and beyond, fitness is perceived as the primary marker for health.

It can buy you more career years, and an additional measure of approbation from younger employees who may well spend the weekends mountain biking.

Consider your audience

Starting a sentence with "when I was your age" or "back in the day" invariably leads to a story that's more celebratory of the speaker than applicable to the listener.

It can all be amusing socially. But in a professional setting, "war stories" — especially when told to younger associates — need to provide a specific lesson or insight or example.

There's a distinct line between sharing experiences that help your colleagues and barely concealed self-aggrandizement. The older the self-promoter, the more objectionable the dissertation becomes.

Humility should accompany success. It's an indication of well-earned maturity, an acknowledgement of the opportunity and good fortune that helped make it all possible.

BUCKLE DOWN AND INFLUENCE UP

If you intend to be a leader, you need to communicate with distinction and consistency across a range of opportunities, external and internal.

Within your own organization, you need to "influence up."

At the best of times, it can be difficult for employees with aspirations of leadership to influence up — to get and hold the attention of top management, and then convince them to take a specific course of action.

Influencing up might include selling your directors on a new advertising campaign or additional IT spending or your promotion to the inner circle.

But in difficult economic times, many corporate leaders aren't open to being influenced, from any direction. They're understandably preoccupied with staying competitive, and, in some cases, staying in business.

That can stall the career advancement of those who serve below.

There remains, however, plenty of potential for successful communication up the corporate food chain. By preparing strategically, you can connect confidently with the powers-that-be and influence up.

Here's how.

Do your research

Senior decision-makers are quicker than ever to dismiss or ignore entreaties that don't relate to the most pressing needs of the business, whether short or long-term.

They're more focused than ever. They have to be.

You need to know what's keeping your leaders up at night.

They should be keen to tell you. After all, the more employees who understand the organization's challenges, the better.

Start with those you report to. Ask: "What are your top three priorities?" "How can I best help you achieve them?" "Can you tell me more?"

Attend conferences, corporate town hall meetings, and online forums to find out what your outfit's leaders are thinking, and why. Whenever possible, engage them in friendly but respectful conversation, ensuring that you observe the tenets of organizational protocol.

Don't go too big, too fast. Play your position. Otherwise, you'll alienate the very people you want to influence.

Think "solutions"

Now that you know what's causing your leaders insomnia, can you recommend anything that can help them sleep?

Once, in a downtown coffee shop, I overheard two intense, mid-level staffers complaining to their genial, composed boss about an acute workplace issue. They whined incessantly, lamenting, in melodramatic detail, about how it was affecting their productivity.

Their manager, remarkably restrained under the circumstances, kept asking for suggestions about how the problem might be fixed or even approached, but no ideas were forthcoming.

Indeed, the more junior employees seemed barely to hear him, they were so caught up in their own ordeal.

It was a perfect opportunity to influence up, thrown away.

In tough times especially, leaders at every level are looking for solutions.

Can you provide them? Any thoughts on how operations in your division can be conducted more efficiently? Has a longtime customer provided you with feedback that can help your sales team attract more clients? Do you have a killer concept for a social media initiative that can reach a younger demographic?

Bring them on.

Be definitive

You're ready to present your ideas to your leaders, but will they listen?

Unambiguous purpose and language will go a long way to ensuring they do. Both deliver extraordinary impact, especially in difficult times.

The longer you spend lamenting how bad things are, the less authority you'll be able to muster.

The more time you spend proposing workable solutions, the more consideration and respect you'll gain.

Convey your observations, recommendations, and next steps clearly and succinctly, without getting bogged down in the quagmire of minutia.

Anticipate those difficult questions

Nothing will undermine your influence with senior leadership faster than an inability to defend your rationale and answer tough, probing questions. Prepare tight, to-the-point responses, and determine to conclude your communication positively, leaving your listeners wanting to hear from (and deal with) you again.

Even if your plan or initiative gets rejected, you need to have established areas of common interest and agreement, so you'll be welcomed back with a new concept another day.

Stay optimistic

Optimism doesn't mean naïveté. On the contrary, it means embracing the realistic conviction that, while economic conditions may not be great, they'll eventually get better. They always do.

It means conveying an upbeat, constructive attitude when communicating up and down the organization. Your leaders will notice.

It's easy to be pessimistic. Instead, express optimism.

Remember my uncle's advice

The day after I graduated from university, as I was about to begin my career in journalism, my uncle took me aside and delivered some firm words of advice. He said, "Make your boss look good."

It was 1973. Regretfully, I didn't always follow that sage counsel, with predictably bad results. But when I did, it worked marvellously.

Make your boss look good. It's the ultimate way of influencing up.

ON BEARING BAD NEWS

To speak like a leader, you'll have to deliver bad news on occasion.

How you communicate it can be as significant as the news itself. Indeed, those who convey such information with poise and integrity can make an impression that endures long after the effects of the originating event.

Bad news will come, sooner or later.

Here's how to communicate it when it does.

Take the initiative

A major indicator of career and life maturity is a person's willingness to openly confront difficult situations, refusing to hide behind the easily erectable barriers of voicemail, email, and absenteeism.

Confident, secure executives acknowledge bad news, consider how it will affect their customers and employees, and then get busy contacting them.

For example, investment advisors who call their clients in a market meltdown to provide perspective and assurance will likely enjoy the benefits of a continued business relationship.

Conversely, a broker who can't be located in a crash likely won't.

Be direct

People want their bad news straight, without equivocation or patter. So get right to it.

Relate the facts, explain what they mean to your listeners, and then leave plenty of time for dialogue.

Your audience may be alarmed by information in the media that, upon scrutiny, isn't objective or even accurate. In such cases, you need to filter out the errant material and ensure a common understanding of the facts. Things may be better than they were first led to believe.

That being said, the worst thing you can do is to communicate good or positive news first, in an attempt to mitigate the unpleasant tidings to come. Your listeners are bound to feel resentful.

Answer questions forthrightly, but avoid alarmist, over-the-top language ("It's a nightmare out there") that can instantly undermine hard-won rapport.

Listen carefully

Hurting, fearful people need to express their anxieties. Listen to them do it.

The ability to listen to others — quietly, calmly, and without frequent interruptions and distractions — qualifies as one of your best communication tools.

First-rate leaders listen extraordinarily well. They know that nothing binds them to their audience like the patient, respectful act of listening.

Be calm

Panic is contagious. Your audience will discern alarm in your voice, so keep it out.

Your listeners may raise their voices, but you can't raise yours. If they're angry and need to vent their emotions, let them.

Anger is virtually impossible to sustain for extended

periods, so when they calm down, all parties involved will be ready for a composed, reasoned conversation.

Empathize

Bad news, whether it's the loss of a job or the plummeting value of an investment portfolio, can be tough to receive. Failure to recognize that fact is a certain way to bring about estrangement.

Your words need to be sincere, specific, and brief. Be empathetic, without going overboard. The "I feel your pain" stuff is overdone and superficial.

If appropriate, apologize

If you've made an error that's contributed to the situation at hand, acknowledge the mistake and fully apologize — once.

Make sure, though, that it's a *real* apology.

Employ one of the most powerful combinations of words in the English language: "I'm sorry. Please forgive me."

Increasingly, public figures don't apologize. They've become masters of the partial or semi-apology, reflecting the values of a society where accepting responsibility for individual actions has diminished. In the process, we've created a catalogue of expedient talk-show rationales for our shortcomings.

Progressive leaders know that stonewalling is never the way to go; it has a short, unsustainable shelf life.

They know that once a mistake has been made and an apology sincerely expressed, most recipients are remarkably gracious. The quick, forthright admission of an error doesn't weaken credibility, it strengthens it.

Provide next steps

You've delivered the bad news. You've discussed the bad news. Now, move on.

Provide your listeners with a well-considered answer to the question, "Where do we go from here?" by recommending a clear strategy, representing one or more steps or initiatives.

Elementary or complex, the strategy needs to be communicated in an encouraging manner, even if the short-term outlook remains problematic.

Usually, how you finish delivering bad news will remain more important to your audience than how you start.

But then, finishing strong has always been the mark of a leader.

COMMUNICATING IN A CRISIS

Speaking like a leader runs the gamut, from communicating in the best of times to the worst.

It's how you conduct yourself in the bad times that will do more to influence others' opinion of you, than how you behave when all's well with the world.

An astonishing number of senior executives and officials in business and government still haven't clued into that reality. Many still don't seem to understand the basics of effective crisis communication.

It doesn't matter if you run a city or a convenience store: In a crisis the people you serve — your constituents, your employees, and your customers — will look to you for assurance, for direction, for connection. You need to be there to provide it.

If you're not there, there's a vacuum, and an unsettling combination of angst and uncertainty can settle in.

What successful emergency response comes down to, according to a commonly used crisis communication mantra, is "doing the next right thing."

What are those next right things? Here are four steps of crisis communication response you need to heed.

Be visible

As a leader in a crisis, you need to be seen and heard.

Take, for example, Rudy Giuliani, who, as mayor

of New York City, set the modern benchmark for crisis communication following the terrorist attacks of September 11, 2001.

Giuliani understood that he not only had to lead from the outset, but that he had to be *seen* leading.

He communicated early and often. He was everywhere and used the media as his conduit to millions.

But Giuliani didn't go it alone, and neither should you.

When possible, involve those who can help you tell your story with full credibility. Perhaps it's an official, a subject matter expert, or a customer to help fill in the gaps in your own knowledge and experience.

Remember that in a crisis, visuals — a face, a flag — take on tremendous emotional power. Use appropriate images to build your narrative.

Act fast

Whatever the event, your reputation as a leader increases or diminishes in direct proportion to the time it takes you to respond — publicly — with boldness and sensitivity.

Crisis communication professionals often tell their clients that in the opening stages of an emergency they'll never have all the information they need, but that there's really no choice. They must communicate. Silence or absence will be taken as incompetence, disinterest, or even an admission of guilt.

Inform your stakeholders — employees, clients, suppliers, officials, shareholders — as well as the media that you're on the case with an early statement: "This is what we know. This is what we're doing about the situation. This is how we'll keep you informed of developments."

Control the message

You simply cannot communicate too frequently in a crisis. When there's a dearth of information, rumours abound.

Make it your goal to provide reliable, comprehensive updates.

Delay, obfuscate, or dither, and your stakeholders — who crave strong leadership — will first be bewildered, then disappointed, and finally angry.

Be willing to take your lumps in the media but don't be a doormat. Aggressively correct inaccuracies in any news reports, lest they cause confusion and anxiety among your audiences.

Be human

A crisis reveals the mettle of an organization and, often, the character of the person who leads it. If your emergency involves loss of life or suffering, you need to speak openly and caringly about the tragedy.

Compassion is essential. Not your style? That's too bad, because it's an integral part of the deal.

Your organization may survive a badly-handled crisis but you may not. It can kill your career.

SPEAKING *THROUGH* THE MEDIA

We live in a media world.

You need to know how to excel in it.

As someone who has prepared hundreds of senior executives, physicians, and public figures for media interviews, I can tell you that, like giving a great presentation, communicating successfully with reporters comes down to a simple principle: making it about your audience.

And your audience isn't the reporter who's interviewing you. It's those the media serves — consumers, customers, taxpayers, homeowners, voters, patients, students, seniors, and children.

You need to be speaking *through* the media to identifiable members of that audience.

Invariably, when executives stumble in their dealings with journalists, it's because they've made the interaction too much about themselves and not nearly enough about their listeners.

Focus on the benefits you and your organization bring to specific members of that audience and you'll vastly increase your odds of generating the coverage you covet.

The following steps will help you communicate effectively through the media.

Be proactive

Do your research. Learn who reports on your industry, sector, or discipline at key news organizations, including online sites. Develop relationships with those journalists. Don't contact them only when there's something in it for you; make a point of updating reporters on developments and trends that could enrich their coverage.

Be accessible

This is huge. Most executives are only too pleased to speak with reporters when they have good news to relate, but somehow disappear when the going gets rocky.

Leaders tell their good news with enthusiasm and their bad news with candor.

However you play it, the media will get its story anyway, sooner or later, with or without you. That's why it's in your best interests to open the "front door" to journalists, meeting them, if possible, face-to-face, and outlining your position in a logical, rational manner. If you refuse to open the door, reporters won't simply go away. They'll walk around to the side door or crawl through a back window.

Deal openly and honestly with reporters and there'll be no need for journalistic break-and-enters. That doesn't mean the coverage you receive will always be complimentary or even fair. You can't control the media, no one can. But what you can do is ensure that your position is clearly explained and understood — in good times and bad.

Be clear

Reporters and editors are swamped with information, much of it useless and some of it incomprehensible. They spend much of their time attempting to bring clarity and understanding to complex, perplexing issues. The last thing they need is another confusing story or story pitch. Besides, they won't always have time to figure out your deal. That's your job.

Make your outreach to the media "tight and bright."

As an example, let's consider the successful story pitch of a pharmaceutical company seeking to generate media coverage — and therefore patient demand — for its newest drug.

The pitch is organized according to that old reliable Power of Three.

First comes the context: "More than two million Canadians suffer from this disease."

Second come the benefits: "A medication has recently been approved to help those with the illness live healthier, more active, and more productive lives."

Finally, there's the call to action: "Two patients who participated in the clinical trial for the medication say it's literally changed their lives. They'd like to share their story."

Be realistic

If you're looking to create coverage, you need a healthy dose of perspective.

The opening of your new pet store in Hooterville doesn't qualify as a national story, unless Paris Hilton has agreed to manage it. Have reasonable expectations of coverage while making the most of your realistic opportunities with local, trade, and industry media.

Consider innovative ways to make your pitch more appealing — can you arrange a good photo opportunity? Pets and children make for compelling visuals. Does your store feature an unusual animal or display? Will the Mayor be attending the official opening? Think about the image you want the media to perceive, and then begin constructing it.

Never push

If a reporter declines to cover your story, thank her for considering it and move on. Don't even think about arguing the point. Journalists almost never reverse their decisions, and if you do push, you run the risk of alienating an important contact.

Conduct your media relations for the long term. It works best that way.

Top Ten Media Tips

1. **Take time to prepare**

   Never speak to a reporter without adequate preparation. If you have to buy time, do it. Even a few minutes of prep can make a big difference. Rehearse your responses to the difficult questions you'll likely receive. Create a one-page background sheet for the journalist, outlining your issue or initiative in simple terms, with all relevant names, titles, and definitions (for scientific, financial, and technical terms) included. If you have to use jargon, make sure you explain what it means.

2. **Take the initiative**

   Place a time limit on the interview. Get your story out right away. If you're interrupted, pick it up as soon as you're able.

3. **Bridge the credibility gap**

   Be able to support your story with examples, statistics, and third-party endorsements.

Reporters are notoriously skeptical, and rightly so. It's up to you, not the journalist, to bridge the credibility gap.

4. **Consider your demeanour**
   Look at the reporter as if he or she is a friend you like and respect. Be engaged. Maintain eye contact and stay focused. Never smile if the news is bad, especially if death or injury is involved.

5. **Brand strategically**
   When you're providing positive information, name your organization. When the news is negative, say "we" or "this company."

6. **Be human**
   Empathize. Sympathize. If it's appropriate, apologize. Demonstrate genuine concern for others. Be sensitive. Be real.

7. **Maintain your cool**
   Some reporters will be confrontational. It's simply an interviewing technique and rarely personal. Firmly but politely bridge back to your story and maintain your composure.

8. **Never say "no comment"**
   In addition to sounding terrible, it's become a tired cliché. And increasingly, journalists are taking it to mean that you're guilty of something.

9. **Don't go "off the record"**

   There's no such thing anymore: if an off the record comment is hot enough, the reporter will use it — and burn you.

10. **Be confident**

    You're the expert. You should look, sound, and act like it. Sometimes, there's a fine line between confidence and arrogance. Don't cross it. Reporters will be there, waiting to deflate you if you do.

WHAT LEADERS DO

Consider this story. Our meeting was coming to an end.

"I'm going to get out of here and let you get back to work," I said to the managing partner of a leading international law firm, as we sat in his New York office.

"Let me walk you downstairs," he replied.

"Oh no, you don't have to do that," I protested.

"I want to," he said.

As we made our way through his firm's headquarters, everyone we encountered smiled and said hello, and it wasn't because I was there.

We took the elevator down to the lobby, where my client — who makes more in a year than the annual gross domestic product of a small Baltic country — walked with me to the doors of the midtown

Manhattan building, shook my hand, and said, "Thank you for your help."

How long did it all take him? Including the walk and the elevator ride, down and back up, perhaps ten minutes.

But his courtesy continues to make an impact on me.

Accomplished, and much more

As a communication skills coach, I'm privileged to work with leaders in Canada and the United States. They're accomplished in their respective fields, of course, but that's not what impresses me most. It's how they make the people around them feel. It's how they create and enhance relationships.

It's what they, as leaders, do.

It's been said that the higher you go in an organization, the better the interpersonal skills of those you meet. I'm sure there are exceptions, but in my experience it's proven to be true.

Now here's an opportunity for you: because so few people in business, government, and education conduct themselves like gracious, self-assured leaders, it's easy to stand out, to make your mark and build a loyal, trusted network of friends, colleagues, and supporters.

Building a network is important because no one achieves great success, and maintains it, without the help of others. Smart leaders know that. It's why they devote so much time and energy to their relationships. The payoffs, both tangible and emotional, of a strong network are out of all proportion to the investment involved.

Here's what leaders do to engage others. You can do the same.

Leaders give back

Without exception, the leaders I know are immensely thankful for their good fortune — their opportunities, their families, and their health. And so they give back.

They volunteer on charitable boards, contribute to community causes, and serve as mentors and advisors. As their outreach widens, so, correspondingly, does their influence.

When you do good things, great things happen.

Leaders express appreciation

The leaders I know are quick to express thanks for what they consider to be a job well done. Once, a client recommended that I dine at a certain restaurant in Old Montreal. I visited the establishment, and had a terrific meal. But when I went to pay, the server informed me that the bill had been taken care of — by my client.

The tab was $150, and while I greatly appreciated the dinner, what I was most grateful for was the thought behind the gesture.

You don't have to buy someone a meal to deepen a relationship. If you come across a book you think a colleague would enjoy, send it off with a handwritten note. If you're on a budget, just do the note.

The best investment a prospective leader can make is in high-end stationery. It will say a lot about you.

Leaders stay connected

The successful leaders I know "ping" regularly, initiating quick email and voicemail contact with the members of their network. A message might consist of a note of congratulations, a heads-up that they're going to be in town, or just a friendly hello.

As busy as they are, they rarely permit an email to go unanswered. They almost never drop the communication ball.

Leaders assume the responsibility of replying promptly to correspondence, even when there's no benefit in it for them.

Interestingly, and tellingly, the lower you go down the corporate food chain, the more emails go unanswered. By failing to respond, the recipients are nevertheless sending a negative message about themselves.

Leaders create supporters

In 2007, a client of mine had a couple of extra tickets to a black-tie dinner, and invited me to attend, with a guest. I asked a friend to come along.

At the time, she was working on a professional designation, and shared that fact with my client. He wished her well, and that was that. Or so she thought.

A year later, my friend earned her designation. Her name and photograph appeared in the newspaper, along with others who had successfully completed the course.

Soon after, she told me that my client, whom she had met only the once at the dinner the year before, had sent her a letter of congratulations on her achievement.

My friend was thrilled and my client has a fan for life.

When she told me about the letter I was pleased, but not surprised.

"That's what leaders do," I said.

Final Words

My father was dying and he knew it. I knew it, too.

It was the early afternoon of Saturday, May 8, 1999.

James Goode "Jimmy" Gray had been battling congestive heart and lung problems for the better part of a year. Now, he was fading quickly.

I had seen that for myself, earlier in the week, after flying to Nova Scotia to visit him in the Intensive Care Unit of the hospital. There, I found not a dashing former athlete but an impersonator, a pale, frail old man, nearing the end.

I returned to Toronto, hoping for a life-saving operation, anything that would save my father. But when I called on May 8, I knew he wasn't going to make it. We talked. He was tired. I began to break down.

"What's wrong?" he asked. "What's wrong?"

I choked out the words, "You know I love you."

With the startling formality of so many men of his generation, he replied, "Oh yes, yes. But you must carry on."

Our conversation was brief. It was to be the last time we spoke. Sitting at home, alone and distraught, I beat down my emotions and began to think more calmly, rationally.

"What can I possibly do," I asked myself, "to make my father feel better today?"

And then, like a bolt of lightning, came the answer: Paul Henderson, the Canadian hockey legend.

Henderson comes through in the clutch

I've known Henderson since 1995, when I was introduced to his Christian ministry, the LeaderImpact group. When I called him at home and asked him to phone my dad, whom he had met briefly the year before, there was no hesitation.

And so Henderson called my father, and they talked and laughed and prayed together. And for the remaining few days of his life, my father would ask everyone who visited his hospital room, "Guess who called me?"

And the guest would naturally reply, "I don't know. Who?"

Dad would pause, but only slightly. Then, with extraordinary timing and delivery, he'd say, "The hero of '72, Paul Henderson."

I don't know if it was due to the phone call from Henderson or not, but my brothers told me that a peace had come over my dad. I think he knew his future was assured.

More than five hundred people attended my father's funeral.

Henderson doesn't talk about their conversation. It remains highly personal, privileged information, like so much of what's disclosed to the former hockey star.

"People get referred to me who are not doing well," he says.

Paul Henderson has lived significantly longer since scoring the "Goal of the Century" than he had before it. On September 28, 1972, in a storybook, come-from-behind finish, he potted his own rebound with thirty-four seconds left in the eighth and final game of the Summit Series against the former Soviet Union to win the competition for Canada.

The nation went crazy for Henderson, then twenty-nine "with an edge."

The instant, overwhelming fame that arrived with the goal didn't dull the edge — it sharpened it. Despite fame, financial security, and the love of his wife and children, he often felt restless and disconnected. Returning to the Toronto Maple Leafs and the National Hockey League, he bowed to the new expectations of fans and teammates and began to overreach. His relationship with team owner Harold Ballard, already fractious, turned poisonous.

"I didn't know how to handle the anger and bitterness," says Henderson. "But I was smart enough to know that something was missing. It took me three years to find it."

What he found was a set of spiritual beliefs that has fuelled his life since 1975.

Henderson the encourager

"There's so much I don't understand," he says. "I don't understand why a mother in her late thirties with two children gets breast cancer and dies. I don't understand why kids are abducted and killed. But what I do know is that life is all about helping others. I'm an encourager — I want to make my life count."

That he has done. Among his accomplishments, Henderson has established more than seventy men's groups throughout southern Ontario. They meet weekly to discuss spiritual matters, matters of the heart.

While expressing much more satisfaction with his life since 1972 than before it, Henderson remains deeply proud of his heroics in the Summit Series. Incredibly, he scored the winning goal in each of the final three games.

At times he appears almost awed by the manner in which his hockey legend has been sustained and nurtured. When he speaks at high schools, he receives standing ovations from kids who were born many years after the famous goals, their memories forged by their parents and by heart-stopping video.

An exceptional presenter, Henderson often jokes that he "played too many years without a helmet."

That line always gets a big laugh.

However, when he speaks of being a Canadian, you can hear a pin drop.

"We, as Canadians, don't celebrate many things," he says, "but we celebrate our hockey. I'm immensely proud to be a Canadian. We won the lottery, being able to live in this country."

How leaders speak is important, and what leaders do matters a great deal.

But what leaders *are*, that's the main thing.

Paul Henderson proves the point.

About the Author

Jim Gray is a speaker, communication skills coach, and media strategist based in Toronto. For more than twenty years he has conducted media and presentation skills sessions with senior executives, physicians, and public figures throughout Canada and the United States.

"I'm proud to be a storyteller," says Gray. "I help my clients cut through the information clutter to create and communicate stories that are clear, concise, and meaningful."

The principal of Media Strategy Inc., Gray plans and implements communication strategies for clients across a range of sectors. A former journalist with the *Toronto Star* and the CBC, he frequently provides counsel to organizations facing challenging public and internal issues.

Gray delivers keynote presentations on "How Leaders Speak," The Power of the Story," "Communicating in a Crisis," "Influence Up," and "The Generation Trap."

He serves on the faculty of the Canadian Management Centre and contributes articles on communication to the *Globe and Mail*. Gray is a graduate of Acadia University in Nova Scotia.

His website is *www.jimgray.ca*.

Index

Dundurn Books of Related Interest

Before You Say Yes …
A Guide to the Pleasures and
Pitfalls of Volunteer Boards
by Doreen Pendgracs
978-1-55488-703-3
$19.99

Doreen Pendgracs shares valuable
information from her twenty-five years
of experience sitting on various boards
of directors in an easy-to-understand,
conversational style. Pendgracs leads the reader through
the intricacies of management style, board etiquette, and
financial obligations, creating a full picture of what you need
to know before agreeing to serve on any kind of board.

Saris on Scooters
How Microcredit Is Changing
Village India
by Sheila McLeod Arnopoulos
978-1-55488-722-4
$29.99

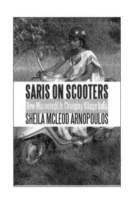

Renowned author and journalist
Sheila McLeod Arnopoulos uses
her talent for investigative reporting
to take us deep into the poorest
villages in India. Yet, far from being passive victims of their
circumstances, the women who live there have joined forces
and are making astute use of microcredit to break the cycle
of poverty. After witnessing these women's inspiring success
stories first-hand, Arnopoulos has come to believe that such
villages have a potential strength equal to that of modern,
high-tech cities in India.

Kickstart
How Successful Canadians
Got Started
by Alexander Herman,
Paul Matthews, and Andrew Feindel
978-1-55002-783-9
$26.99

Kickstart profiles more than thirty
prominent Canadians, including a
professional athlete (former CFL star
Norman Kwong), a TV personality (Valerie Pringle), a
Native leader (Matthew Coon Come), and a former prime
minister (Brian Mulroney). Their collective wisdom, offered
in their own words, just might help readers "kickstart" their
own lives and careers.

Available at your favourite bookseller.

DUNDURN PRESS
w w w . d u n d u r n . c o m